MARRIED TO
JESUS

MATTHEW J. WHITE

To my wife, Anne,
for loving me and forgiving me daily.

Table of Contents

Forward

Every time I perform a wedding, I remind the congregation that we are participating in something of a mystery. I invite them to keep their eyes peeled for the glory of God. I believe God loves weddings because there may be nowhere else in our world where He can be more clearly seen than in a marriage. It is no coincidence Jesus began his public ministry at a wedding, turning water into wine.

Matt White is still young, and his relationship with his wife, Anne, is still growing. But Matt has recognized the mystery. He calls us not only to invite Jesus into our marriages but to allow Jesus to love through us. Matt has captured a simple and profound call.

So, I invite you to sit with this book and let it lead you deeper into the mystery. Allow it to help you develop eyes to see the glory of God, even in your own home.

Joe Coffey, Lead Pastor
Hudson Community Chapel
Hudson, Ohio

Preface

*"Have I not commanded you? Be strong and courageous. Do not
be terrified; do not be discouraged, for the LORD your God will
be with you wherever you go." (Joshua 1:9)*

I used to dream of going to the Olympics. Growing up, my
wall was plastered with ribbons, medals and pictures of my
accomplishments as a young gymnast at Metroplex Gymnastics
in Dallas, Texas. Early on in my gymnastics career, I knew this
is what I was meant to do. I started in the fifth grade, and by the
time I was in seventh grade, I had given up every other sport in
order to focus on gymnastics.

I can't say for sure when it was, but sometime in junior
high, I made a list of three goals that I was destined to reach.

　　　1. Qualify for nationals.

　　　2. Get a scholarship to college.

　　　3. Go to the Olympics.

A few years after I made this list, I qualified and competed
at the Junior National gymnastics competition in Osh Kosh,
Wisconsin. A couple years later, I won a scholarship to

compete on the team at Kent State University in Kent, Ohio. (At the time, I had no clue what the phrase "four dead in Ohio" meant!) If you know much about men's gymnastics, and even if you don't, you probably would know that Kent State was not the mecca for breeding Olympians. It was a decent team, and I was a decent gymnast.

Needless to say, I never made it to the Olympics. The closest I came to the Olympics was through a few guys I knew of that I competed against at Ohio State. Notice I said "knew of;" I didn't even know them, just knew *of* them. And, my coach back at Metroplex is now one of the coaches for several Olympians.

I didn't accomplish 100 percent of my goals. Two out of three ain't bad, right? Or does that mean I'm a failure because I didn't accomplish what I set out to do? I don't believe so. I tried my very best, and in many regards I was very successful in my efforts. That's what God wants, our very best effort.

We are called to be imitators of Christ, in life and in marriage. It is important, though, to realize that this book attempts to address the ideal marriage – one that emulates the relationship of Christ and the church. Every marriage on earth falls short of that ideal, even Christian marriages. But God makes one promise: that Christ is in us and provides us with the hope of glory. Whatever your failures or mistakes, you can begin today to live out the ideal Christian marriage by depending on the power of the Holy Spirit within you.

As we gain a deeper understanding of God's ideal for marriage, many will see the stark contrast with our own marriages. The world will try to use that contrast to make you think, "I'm a failure as a husband or wife. My marriage can never reflect that ideal."[1] But, as God told Joshua not to be discouraged as he prepared to cross the Jordan to enter the Promised Land, God also encourages us in that "the Lord your God will be with you wherever you go."[2]

I worked very hard to succeed in gymnastics, and although I didn't reach the Olympics, my efforts were rewarded – I met the love of my life at Kent State. Some may say hitting two out of three of my goals isn't bad. I say the third goal just changed during the process.

So, let us focus on the ideal, and then by God's power strive to attain it.

Chapter One

To Be Like Jesus

"Be imitators, therefore, as dearly loved children and live a life of love, just as Christ loved us and gave himself up for us as a fragrant offering and sacrifice to God." (Ephesians 5:1-2)

It was the late 80s. Big hair was in. The first George Bush was president. And the band *U2* was on its rise to the top of the charts. My older brother, Jeremy, had gotten me hooked on this little band from Ireland. They were the coolest thing around. My idol at the time was the drummer of *U2*, Larry Mullen Jr. His calm, cool demeanor. His spiked hair and white t-shirt and jeans. He was cool, and I wanted to be cool, too.

If you'd look at my eight or ninth grade class picture, you'd realize how much I wanted to be like Larry Mullen Jr. I had the spiked hair, the white t-shirt, and of course the calm, cool demeanor (although you might not be able to see that part in the picture). All things considered, me and Mr. Mullen were almost twins!

Is that all it takes to be like someone? To look, dress and act like them? When I think back, I really wasn't anything like this guy. I didn't play the drums. I wasn't Irish. I wasn't traveling the world performing for audiences of tens of thousands. And, to my frustration, I wasn't nearly as cool as he was. Today, I realize that if you truly respect and admire someone, and you want to become more like that person, you have to get to know him. You need to understand his personality and find out why he does the things he does. Just by looking or behaving like someone from the outside does not make you "like" that person.

So, what does it mean then to be *like* Jesus? Paul put it this way in Colossians:

> *Whatever you do, in word or deed, do everything in the name of the Lord Jesus, giving thanks to God the Father through him.*[1]

That pretty much says it all right there, doesn't it? To be like Christ, we must do "everything" in His name. Every word, every deed. There's nothing to read between the lines, no questions. Paul says in Ephesians that we are specifically called

13

to "be imitators" of Jesus. To be like Christ then means to make decisions as if Jesus was in your place. Jesus said he has set an "example that you should do as I have done for you."[2]

People's Mistakes are God's Purposes

I heard an aphorism recently that I really liked: "People's mistakes are God's purposes." That little five word phrase says a great deal about the difference in how we perceive our circumstances in life and how God looks at things.

In preparing for this book, this concept of imitating Jesus has proven much harder than it originally sounded. Even in the little things, I make decisions I know Jesus wouldn't make. I go a few miles over the speed limit. I avoid people that I know could use a hand or someone to talk to. I take a second glance at the cover of that magazine in the line at the grocery store. All things that I know are wrong, but for whatever reason I do anyway.

Paul said it best when he said, "For what I do is not the good I want to do; no, the evil I do not want to do—this I keep on doing."[3] It's difficult to comprehend. Why is it that I do the things that I know I shouldn't do? It's because of sin and my selfish desire to please myself or others, not God. From the

14

very beginning of time, God allowed us to make choices. And, the first choices that led to sin in the Garden of Eden lead to the sins I commit today.

But that's just the beginning of the story. After many, many years, God sent his son, Jesus Christ, who ultimately died a sacrificial death, so that I could be free from my sins. Now, that doesn't mean I don't sin, because I do. What it does mean is that by the grace of God, I am forgiven of my sins. Even when I keep doing what I know is wrong, God is faithful and will forgive me if I ask for his forgiveness. (If you want to know more about what all this means, see the section in the back of this book called *Know Jesus*)

Then what do we do with all this information? How can we get past the fact that we'll never be perfect? We strive for righteousness. We become imitators of Christ. We try to live a life according to the way Jesus would live if he was here in our shoes. So, where do we start? We start by getting to know Jesus better. We learn about him and what he said and did, and more importantly...why. And, then, we imitate him. We attempt to integrate Jesus' character into our lives, into the things we do day in and day out – at work, with our kids, in social settings, and most importantly, in our marriage.

Jesus had a good deal to say about relationships. First he established the priority of relationships. "Anyone who loves his father or mother more than me is not worthy of me; anyone who loves his son or daughter more than me is not worthy of me."[4] God is saying that he comes first. We are not to love anyone more than God.

But, then, he very specifically declares that the relationship between a husband and wife is the second most important relationship we can have. He compares the marriage relationship to that of Christ's relationship with the church, his chosen people. The best description I have found in the Bible about marriage is in the fifth chapter of Ephesians: (For those of you who have your hang-ups about the "s" word – submit – I'll talk more about this later.)

> *Submit to one another out of reverence for Christ.*
> *Wives, submit to your husbands as to the Lord. For the*
> *husband is the head of the wife **as Christ** is the head of*
> *the church, his body, of which he is the Savior. Now as*
> *the church submits to Christ, so also wives should*
> *submit to their husbands in everything. Husbands, love*
> *your wives, **just as Christ** loved the church and gave*

*himself up for her to make her holy, cleansing her by
the washing with water through the word, and to
present her to himself as a radiant church, without
stain or wrinkle or any other blemish, but holy and
blameless.* **In this same way,** *husbands ought to love
their wives as their own bodies. He who loves his wife
loves himself. After all, no one ever hated his own
body, but he feeds and cares for it,* **just as Christ does**
*the church— for we are members of his body. For this
reason a man will leave his father and mother and be
united to his wife, and the two will become one flesh.
This is a profound mystery—but I am talking about*
Christ and the church. *However, each one of you also
must love his wife as he loves himself, and the wife
must respect her husband.*[5]

The emphasis is mine, as I intend to call out the fact that in
just twelve verses, Paul mentions five times that we need to
imitate Christ in our marriage. "As Christ" means "as Christ."
We should treat our spouse as he or she would be treated by
Christ. This is not a simple, one-time event; it is an every day
struggle. It's not easy to act "as Christ" in every situation. In

fact, it's notably difficult. Even though we have been forgiven of our sins and strive to live a life like Christ, we still live in this world and must fight the temptations to do what feels good.

A Permanent Helper

Now, this brings up a challenging point that I struggled with in writing this book. All that has been said so far makes the assumption that you are a believer in Jesus Christ, the living son of God. Does that mean that the principles discussed in this book don't apply if you're not a Christian? I don't believe so. If you truly attempt to actively integrate the character of Jesus into your marriage, there will be beneficial results.

However, the challenges will be much greater for someone outside of a personal relationship with Jesus Christ. Without this relationship, you're on your own. As Christians, we have the Holy Spirit as a permanent helper to depend on when times get tough. And it will most likely get tough at some point.

> ...the Holy Spirit, whom the Father will send in my
> name, will teach you all things and will remind you of
> everything I have said to you. Peace I leave with you;
> my peace I give you. I do not give to you as the world

gives. Do not let your hearts be troubled and do not be afraid.[6]

Acting like Jesus, whether you truly believe or not, will make a difference in your marriage. But, once you can depend on the Holy Spirit, it's a totally different story. We must let him fill our thoughts, let him live in our relationships, so he can stand along side us and encourage us as we strive to be like Christ.[7]

The Character of Christ

What was Jesus like? What are the attributes we should be imitating? If we are to do everything in his name, what does that look like? As a fun and helpful exercise, I asked several people to give me single words that described Jesus. Think about that for a minute or two. What words pop into your head? Here are a few that came up:

Humble	Righteous	Selfless
Obedient	Submissive	Trustworthy
Welcoming	Encourager	Example
Comforting	Redeemer	Eternal

19

Faithful	Loving	King
Amazing	Sacrifice	Savior
Perfect	Sinless	Patient
Forgiving	Merciful	Just
Kind	Complete	Compassionate
Holy	Honest	Infinite
Almighty	Omniscient	Leader
Teacher	Servant	Friend

Now, there are several here that I can mark off the list that I will never be. We've already established that I'm not perfect. I'm pretty sure I'm not omniscient, righteous or eternal. And, unless I buy an island somewhere and name myself supreme leader of that land, I'm fairly confident I will not be a king at any point in my lifetime.

But, what I can imitate are attributes like showing compassion and kindness, being humble and faithful. I can be honest, merciful and patient. I can strive to live a life of servanthood and sacrifice. Galatians 5:22-23 says, "the fruit of the Spirit is love, joy, peace, patience, kindness, goodness, faithfulness, gentleness and self-control. Against such things there is no law."[8]

In Paul's letter to the Colossians, he said:

> *Therefore, as God's chosen people, holy and dearly loved, clothe yourselves with compassion, kindness, humility, gentleness and patience. Bear with each other and forgive whatever grievances you may have against one another. Forgive **as the Lord** forgave you. And over all these virtues put on love, which binds them all together in perfect unity.*[9]

These are the characteristics Jesus displayed in his years on earth. These are the characteristics we should be imitating in our daily lives.

Almost all these words that describe Jesus can be summed up in one word: Love. Jesus himself said, "A new command I give you: Love one another. As I have loved you, so you must love one another. By this all men will know that you are my disciples, if you love one another."[10]

A Perfect Example

Jesus was the perfect example of the ideal husband or wife. Imagine if you displayed these characteristics each and every

21

day in your relationship with your spouse. Imagine if the first thing you thought of when you woke up in the morning was, "How can I serve my wife today?" or "What can I do today to make my husband's day better?" or "How can I display love and affection to my spouse in a new way today?" If Jesus was in your place, I believe these are the types of things he would be thinking to start his day.

Loving your spouse like Christ loved the church means ignoring yourself. It means making decisions that won't always be easy. It involves giving up some of the things you enjoy or showing patience even when you're tired and grumpy. It takes sacrifice and selflessness.

Christ showed his love for us, his bride, through the ultimate sacrifice. He experienced torture, beating, whipping, mocking, spitting, and finally death on a cross. Every time I think of Christ's death and sacrifice, I now think of Mel Gibson's "The Passion of the Christ." I can't help but recall those images of Jesus being whipped time and time again. All the blood. All the pain and suffering.

Rick Warren, in his book, *Purpose Driven Life*, described Jesus' sacrifice this way:

...the Son of God was stripped naked, beaten until almost unrecognizable, whipped, scorned and mocked, crowned with thorns, and spit on contemptuously. Abused and ridiculed by heartless men, he was treated worse than an animal.

Then, nearly unconscious, he was forced to drag a cumbersome cross up a hill, was nailed to it, and was left to die the slow, excruciating torture of death by crucifixion. While his lifeblood drained out, hecklers stood by and shouted insults, making fun of his pain and challenging his claim to be God. [11]

And why did he do this? He did it because of his love for us. Jesus said, "My command is this: Love each other as I have loved you. Greater love has no one than this, that he lay down his life for his friends." [12]

Would you be willing to lay down your life for your husband or wife? Would you consider your love for your spouse to be a sacrificial love? And, I don't just mean giving a kidney or donating some blood. Would you endure the pain and suffering Jesus endured out of love for your wife? Can you say

that you would die in order that your husband could live?
That's the kind of marriage Jesus has with his bride. That's the
kind of marriage we should be striving for.

From the Chapter

"Loving your spouse like Christ loved the church means
ignoring yourself. It means making decisions that won't always
be easy. It involves giving up some of the things you enjoy or
showing patience even when you're tired and grumpy. It takes
sacrifice and selflessness."

Bible Verse Reference

John 15:12 – "My command is this: Love each other as I have
loved you."

Question:

What can I do today to start showing the characteristics of Jesus
to my spouse?

Chapter 2

If This...Then This

"For we are God's workmanship, created in Christ Jesus to do good works, which God prepared in advance for us to do."
(Ephesians 2:10)

For all you computer programmers reading this, you know exactly what an "if...then" statement is. For the other 99.9 percent of you, let me explain. The basis of writing a good deal of computer programming code lies within this core phrase: *If (condition) then (statement).* The idea is pretty basic: *IF* a designated condition occurs, *THEN* a designated result happens. *If* something else happens, *then* there's a different result.

If you've not been in the business of dealing with computer programming, you've probably never had a second thought about how the software or games or operating system you use works. But, if you think about it for a second, it makes perfect sense. Even as I write this, the "if...then" formula is at work. *If* I hit the T key, *then* a T is placed on the page. And the same

25

applies for every other letter in this sentence, and the ones before and the ones after.

You may be able to relate to video games. My daughter, Audrey, was given a video game system for Christmas, so now I can actually relate in this way, too. Just think of all the "if...then" programming going on in a single video game. The controller has over ten buttons, each having a different result when pressed. Then, create combinations, and the number of "thens" becomes almost infinite. If you hit the green button three times, then you make a super jump. If you hit the control wand and the red button at the same time, then you dive and swim faster. All these actions had to be created through some sort of "if...then" programming.

God, the Programmer

You might call God the big computer programmer in the sky. God has wired the whole universe as one giant "if...then" statement. And it all starts with his grace.

I think that grace is one of the most difficult concepts of the Bible. God truly gave us a gift for absolutely no other reason than because he loved us. The American Heritage dictionary defines grace as "a favor rendered by one who need not do so."[1]

Why would God bestow grace upon anyone? Why me, in particular? And you may feel the same way. I don't believe we will ever know the answer to this question until we're in heaven and can ask God himself. But, it's not really for us to understand as much as it is for us to believe. That's faith.

What we do know is this:

> *For it is by grace you have been saved, through faith—and this not from yourselves, it is the gift of God—not by works, so that no one can boast. For we are God's workmanship, created in Christ Jesus to do good works, which God prepared in advance for us to do.*[2]

God gave us the *free* gift of grace. Because he loved us, he sacrificed his only son so that we might not die to sin. Instead, we are forgiven and can live with him forever. What an amazing concept! And, this is the beginning of God's ultimate "if…then" statement.

I think this formula works perfectly to describe Ephesians 2:8-10. It's like this:

> *If (God gave us the free gift of grace) then (we are to do good works).*

It really is that simple. How can we show God our appreciation for this gift that we do not deserve? By doing good works that will represent his love to others.

And, it's not the other way around. Some people may try to flip the equation like this:

> *If (we do good works) then (we will receive God's approval and be deserving of his love).*

Why would Jesus have gone through so much for us if we could have just gained his favor by being nice and doing good things for others? This is not the case. Nothing we do will ever cause God to love us more or less. He loves us no matter what. But, what Paul is saying in Ephesians is that we are saved through God's grace, and therefore, or because of this, we need to live out a life of good deeds. In other words, we can show God's grace to others by what we do.

Faith without Works

James, Jesus' half-brother, wrote a small book in the New Testament that talks a good deal about faith and works. His writings on this subject have been challenged over the years by both theologians who are honestly attempting to discern its meaning and by those trying to dismantle the doctrine of the Bible. They question the idea I raised a moment ago: Is it works that earn us grace, or is it grace that causes us to do good works?

I do not believe there is any evidence to support the former. James is attempting to make a point that just having faith by itself is not enough, but rather having faith ought to result in our demonstrating good works.

James begins his discussion on faith and works in this way:

> *What good is it, my brothers, if a man claims to have faith but has no deeds? Can such faith save him? Suppose a brother or sister is without clothes and daily food. If one of you says to him, "Go, I wish you well; keep warm and well fed," but does nothing about his physical needs, what good is it? In the same way, faith by itself, if it is not accompanied by action, is dead.[3]*

Again, I'll use the "if…then" formula.

> *If (we have faith) then (we should perform good*
> *deeds).*

It should be a natural reaction. Like your leg when a nurse or doctor taps that spot on your knee. It automatically results in a designated response or reflex reaction. God made us so that we could perform good works in his name. Good works then become the outward display of our inward commitment and belief.

James goes on to describe a couple of examples of faithful people who performed good deeds to show their faith. Abraham was ready to sacrifice his only son, Isaac, whom God had promised would bear many nations, until God saw through Abraham's actions that he, indeed, believed and was faithful. Rahab, a prostitute, helped two spies that Joshua had sent to explore Jericho. Because of the faith displayed in her actions, Rahab and her family were the only ones God spared in that city.

He then wraps up this section by saying, "As the body without the spirit is dead, so faith without deeds is dead."[4] There is a great song by Rich Mullens, called *Screen Door*. The chorus of that song says exactly what James is talking about.

30

> *It's about as useless as a screen door on a submarine*
> *Faith without works, baby, it just ain't happennin'*
> *One is your right hand, one is your left*
> *It's your light, your guide, your life and your breath*
> *Faith without works, like a song you can't sing*
> *It's about as useless as a screen door on a submarine*
> *Faith without works, like a song you can't sing*
> *It's about as useless as a screen door on a submarine*[5]

Faith and works. The two go hand in hand. You can't have one without the other. Jesus, himself, explained this concept in Matthew.

> *...every good tree bears good fruit, but a bad tree bears bad fruit. A good tree cannot bear bad fruit, and a bad tree cannot bear good fruit...Thus, by their fruit you will recognize them.*[6]

There's not an option here. It doesn't say "most good trees bear good fruit" or "some good trees bear good fruit." In fact, "a good tree *cannot* bear bad fruit." If you are in a relationship

31

with Jesus Christ, you are the good tree that bears good fruit. It's what you're naturally supposed to do.

Another good song example that addresses this idea of faith and works is one by Michael W. Smith. It's called *Give It Away*. One of the verses says this:

> *We can entertain compassion*
> *For a world in need of care*
> *But the road of good intentions*
> *Doesn't lead to anywhere*
> *'cause love isn't love*
> *'til you give it away*
> *You gotta give it away*[7]

Hollywood vs. Holy Wed

John and Cassie had it all. Before they got married, they each had their own successful careers. Cassie even kept her last name because of the notable recognition that went along with it. Their marriage was the biggest event of the year, covered in all the tabloids and even the primetime news shows. This one was going to last. Everyone knew it.

A year later, the couple was still making headlines. Her success continued to grow. His business was even more successful than the year before. The perfect couple was expecting their first child. These two were truly in love.

A peek inside the real lives of Mr. and Mrs. Hollywood revealed a different story. With a child on the way, her modeling career was taking a turn for the worse. And, because of this, he was angry with fewer invitations to the who's who events they used to frequent at least once a week. His business was doing so well, she was now jealous of his success and of what (or who) might be keeping him so late at the office. Her pregnancy was decreasing her sex drive, and his desires were driving her crazy. And, with all this going on, the little things began to eat away at both of them: his snoring; her spending habits; his friends; her chewing noises.

Three months later, the headlines read, "John and Cassie Divorce, State Irreconcilable Differences." Their first mistake: not having room for Christ in their lives. They didn't even accept the "if" of the statement, and, therefore, never got to the "then" of thinking of the other person. Each was so wrapped up in his or her own life and wants and needs that there wasn't a thought of what could be done to serve the other.

While this was a fictional couple, you can fill in the names of these two with just about anyone you read about in the tabloids today. On the other hand, a true example of a marriage infused with grace and founded on the principle of serving others is that of my parents.

I desire to have a marriage like my parents. Married for over 35 years, my mom and dad have been living examples of the love of God. My father has always been the Christian leader, and my mother has respectfully submitted and loved my dad. His love for Christ is mirrored in his love for her, and her love of God and the church is encouraged and supported by him.

Now, I don't know everything that goes on outside of my view, of course. But, as Jesus said, "by their fruit you will recognize them."[8] They are both devoted to and involved with their church in Dallas. And, it's not just for show. For almost thirty years, my father has served as a deacon or an elder. He has taught junior high and high school classes, young adult and home fellowship groups, as well as classes on Biblical money management. His faith has been played out through works in the short-term mission field, both at home and abroad. Growing up, what I remember is that just about every time the church doors were open, my dad was there.

My mom is equally involved in service, both to my dad and the church. She always supported my dad in his work, in raising the children, in our family's involvement in the church. She also serves in many unseen ways, like talking with Son Brannon several times a week, sharing with him the TV Guide schedule for the coming days. Son is a member of their church who has lived with Down's syndrome for all of his more than 60 years. She helps at home, at church, and in the community whenever and however she can.

And, these are just some of the things we can see from the outside. Inside the home, they trade back rubs on a regular basis. They support and pray for each other in their respective careers. They tithe over and above what's expected. They pray for friends, family, and even those they don't know. They counsel; they encourage; they support – each other, as well as those around them. They are blessed, and so am I to have them as parents.

Good Works in Your Marriage

Are you starting to get the point? We have been called to do good works. If we are accepting of God's grace, we should respond automatically with the desire to do good things for those around us. Jesus said the two most important things we can do are to love God and love our neighbor. The closest "neighbor" God has given us is our spouse. So, this is where we should start.

Are you "giving away" love in your marriage? Or is your submarine going down because of its screen door? If you're not matching works with your faith, particularly in your marriage, then I hope the following chapters will help you to discover areas where you can focus on improvement.

These two main concepts – becoming like Jesus and the desire to do so as a natural response to God's wonderful gift of grace – are the basis for my ideas and suggestions on creating a stronger marriage, one that embodies the marriage between Christ and the church.

If you're struggling with the concepts that create this foundation, then I suggest you do one of three things:

1) Read through the first two chapters again, and examine your heart to see where you're struggling;

2) Read the section in the back of this book called *Know Jesus* to discover a true relationship with Jesus Christ; or

3) Write to me at matt@marriedtojesus.com.

From the Chapter

"God gave us the *free* gift of grace. Because he loved us, he sacrificed his only son so that we might not die to sin. Instead, we are forgiven and can live with him forever. What an amazing concept! And, this is the beginning of God's ultimate 'if...then' statement."

Bible Verse Reference

James 2:14-17 – "What good is it, my brothers, if a man claims to have faith but has no deeds? ...faith by itself, if it is not accompanied by action, is dead."

Question:

What are two or three ways I can show my appreciation of the grace God has given me?

Chapter 3
Greater Love

"My command is this: Love each other as I have loved you. Greater love has no one than this, that he lay down his life for his friends." (John 15:12-13)

There's nothing like Blue Bell ice cream. If you're from the south, or if you've somehow managed to experience the delicious, one-of-a-kind taste of Blue Bell vanilla ice cream, you know what I'm talking about. Growing up in Texas, I knew nothing else. Blue Bell was a staple in the White house. Especially when all three of us boys were in our teens, we went through gallons of the stuff on a weekly basis.

Almost every night, all three of us and my dad would have a big milk shake made with Blue Bell. Now, when I say big, I don't just mean in a big cup. We made our shakes in mixing bowls and ate them with a spoon. Andy, Jeremy and Dad liked theirs a little chunky. I liked mine mixed up to where it was almost like soup.

Now, the reason I mention Blue Bell, in particular, is because now I live in Ohio. Apparently, Ohioans don't deserve the "best ice cream in the country" because it hasn't made its way up here yet. A couple months ago, I got a call from my younger brother, Andy, in the middle of the afternoon on a weekday. The reason for his call: to announce that Blue Bell was now being sold at Publix in Greenville, South Carolina, where he lives. That's how good this ice cream is; it warrants a call at any time from anywhere.

When our family makes a trip back to Dallas, one of the things I most look forward to is a Blue Bell milk shake. I'll eat them every day of a visit, sometimes twice a day. I *love* the stuff.

Love comes in all shapes and sizes. My love for Blue Bell ice cream is one type of love. It's a bit of a sick type of love, but a love nonetheless. Other kinds of love may include the love for a particular sports team or the love you have for a pet. When it comes to love in a marriage, there are three main types of love: *eros,* or sexual love; *philia,* or brotherly love; and *agape,* or selfless love.

Expected Love

When we get married, we're expected to be good friends and to enjoy a meaningful sexual relationship. When we say, "I love you," we're saying, "You make me feel good," or "I enjoy being around you," or "I want to have sex with you." These are all positive feelings associated with love in a good marriage.[1]

God intended for marriage, and only marriage, to involve a strong sexual relationship.

> *The wife's body does not belong to her alone, but also to her husband; the husband's body does not belong to him alone but also to his wife.*[2]

Our bodies belong to each other in marriage, and the physical attraction present in a marriage should be built upon a foundation of love. From the moment you said, "I do," you agreed to offer your body to your spouse to be enjoyed by him or her. The level of intimacy reached in a respecting sexual relationship is core to the marriage relationship.

In the same way, you and your spouse should be best friends. I am often saddened to see when husbands and wives are not best friends. If we find our deepest friendships outside of our marriage, there's something missing. You and your spouse should feel comfortable spending time together. You should want to share your hopes and dreams with each other, as

41

well as the pains and fears. It's okay if you're sharing these
things with good friends; but if you're sharing it with others
and not your spouse, that's a sign of trouble.

Anne and I are best friends. We find comfort in each
other's presence. Something I heard a long time ago was that
you know you're truly comfortable with someone when you
can sit in silence with that person and not feel like you have to
say anything. There's something to that. There are times when
we are together, maybe after the kids have gone to bed, when
we can just *be*, without having to speak.

We have some different interests and personalities, but we
share in each other's successes and failures. We each have our
own friends, too, but when it comes down to it, there's no one
who knows each of us better than the other. And that feels
good.

Sacrificial Love

It's very good to have friendship in your marriage and to
experience a strong attraction and sexual relationship with your
spouse. I believe most marriages have at least some of both.
But Christ's love for the church goes beyond this level of love.

His love is a giving, sacrificing, selfless love. It is a love that shows itself in action.[3]

> *But God demonstrates his own love for us in this:*
> *While we were still sinners, Christ died for us.*[4]

Jesus loved and gave, not because we were attractive or shared some interest with him, but simply because he loved us. So he humbled himself, he gave up all his glory to serve us. This is the way we are to love our husbands or wives: Giving ourselves, dying to self, serving our spouse.[5]

A Partnership

After Anne and I got married, we lived in Greenville, South Carolina. We had great jobs. We were involved in a wonderful church. We had a good group of friends. Life was good. In a matter of one month, our lives were turned upside down. In October 1997, Anne's dad, Tom, was diagnosed with esophageal cancer, and the prognosis was not good. The following month, we were excited to find out that Anne was pregnant with our first child.

The waves of emotions during that time were enormous. We became very familiar with the nine-hour drive from Greenville to Fremont, Ohio. Tom's struggle with cancer ended in late June the following year. And in August, Audrey was born. It was an amazing time of sadness and joy.

Living in Greenville at the time put us miles away from all of Anne's family which took its toll on everyone with both Tom's passing and our new addition. And deep down I knew, even without her saying it, that Anne was yearning to go home.

I'll admit, before all this happened, moving back to Ohio was certainly not on the top of my list of things to do. Although I felt Anne was leaning this way, I don't believe I ever brought it up. However, around Thanksgiving of that year Anne mentioned the idea of moving back to Ohio, and without hesitation I agreed it would be the best thing for us.

It comes up often, and people ask why in the world did we move from South Carolina to Ohio. And, although I've never actually given this response (I usually mention Tom's cancer and having a baby and being away from Anne's family), the real answer is, "Because I love my wife."

When we love our spouse as Christ loves the church, amazing things happen. Although some may disagree, living in

44

Northeast Ohio has been wonderful. Anne and I have better jobs. We are involved in a better church. We have an amazing group of friends. And life is great!

It Goes Both Ways

Now, some may say, "Man, he really did sacrifice a lot – moving from beautiful South Carolina to cold and snowy Ohio." But, I can tell you, I have been on the receiving end of sacrificial love a great deal more.

Just one example: In August, 2001, I was part of a major "downsizing" at a large advertising agency in Cleveland. I remember the day well. It was Audrey's third birthday. I was let go first thing in the morning, so I was done with my day by about 10:00 a.m. I remember calling Anne and saying, "I have good news and bad news. The good news is I can make it to Audrey's birthday party at school today. The bad news is the reason I'm so available is because I just lost my job."

To get a better feeling for the situation from Anne's perspective, keep in mind that she was a little over a month pregnant with our second child, and here I was making jokes about not having a job. And, if you've done the math right, you've already figured out that the terror attacks of September

45

11, 2001, were only a month away. The economy was not and would not be in a good situation for a while.

We pulled Audrey out of daycare to save money, and I immediately began looking for work. After three months of tireless searching, there was still nothing for me. Anne, meanwhile, was working her tail off and God was blessing her with her best sales commission levels ever. He truly always takes care of us.

In November, 2001, I decided to start my own business, a one man ad agency. As I look back, I cannot remember a time when Anne did not support me. Sure, there were concerns and questions, but she sincerely believed in me and supported me in this venture.

Starting a business required long hours and kept us back from pursuing some of the things we would have normally done or purchased. This venture required the faith of both of us to endure and persist. And, for almost a year of being totally on my own, God had blessed Anne with quarter after quarter of unforeseen commission levels. She never gave up, even after a couple more years of being married to a small business owner.

If someone were to ask Anne how she could sacrifice so much and deal with all the issues involved with being married to an entrepreneur, I'm pretty confident I know what her answer would be: "Because I love my husband."

The Greatest Love

All three loves are good – eros, philia, and agape – and all three are essential to a strong marriage. But, the greatest love is agape. Agape is a love that gives, a love that does not demand or hold onto rights, but has the good of the other at heart. This is the love we need to work on in our marriage in order for our spouse to feel like he or she is married to Jesus.[6]

Jesus said, "My command is this: Love each other as I have loved you. Greater love has no one than this, that he lay down his life for his friends." Are you loving your spouse by laying down your own life for him or her?[7]

From the Chapter

"All three loves are good – eros, philia, and agape – and all three are essential to a strong marriage. But, the greatest love is agape. Agape is a love that gives, a love that does not demand or hold onto rights, but has the good of the other at heart. This is the love we need to work on in our marriage in order for our spouse to feel like he or she is married to Jesus"

Bible Verse Reference

Romans 5:8 – "But God demonstrates His own love toward us, in that while we were yet sinners, Christ died for us."

Question:

Am I willing to sacrifice anything, even my life, for my spouse?

Chapter 4

A Servant's Heart

"For who is greater, the one who is at the table or the one who serves? Is it not the one who is at the table? But I am among you as one who serves." (Luke 22:27)

Each year the women's ministry at our church puts on a great event in the spring for ladies of the church and their friends and family. The Spring Fling usually brings in hundreds of women and is a tremendous outreach event. The gathering offers a great setting for informal social time along with a formal presentation and some sort of meal and refreshments.

Because this event was created as an outreach for the women of the community, the goal is to allow the women of the church to participate and not have to play a role on the day of the event. So, for many years, the men of the church have served all the women at the Spring Fling.

I had the privilege of serving at this wonderful event a couple years ago. What an amazing opportunity to serve – to serve those women and to serve God. The night is meant for the women, so we set up, help prepare the food, set tables, serve the women dinner, fill empty glasses, remove plates and silverware, clean up, and tear down.

Some might not describe that night as an amazing opportunity. Someone with a servant's heart, though, looks at a night like this as a dream come true. When you serve joyfully, you not only help others, but there is something positive that happens to you, too. It makes you feel good, and it puts you one step closer to becoming like Christ.

Jesus said, "For even the Son of Man did not come to be served, but to serve, and to give his life as a ransom for many."[1]

To become like Christ in our marriage, we must serve as Christ served. This involves putting our husband or wife before ourselves. Men, it means helping out around the house and giving of your time for conversations with your wife; it means not taking that business trip sometimes; it means getting involved with parenting decisions. Women, it means supporting your husband in his career; it means giving him time to himself every once in a while; it means understanding and responding to his sexual needs.

Having a servant's heart – a heart like Christ – in our marriage means manifesting that agape love we discussed in the last chapter. It involves a selfless, sacrificing love. It involves a change in our tendency to want to please ourselves.

Love Deeply in Serving

One of the best books I've ever read is *The Life You've Always Wanted*, by John Ortberg. Through this book I was given a revelation about Jesus and his life of serving that I had never considered. Ortberg says, "When Jesus came as a servant, he was not disguising who God is. He was revealing who God is."[2]

What an awesome statement! Jesus didn't come as a child and a carpenter's son and live a life of serving to hide the fact that he was the son of God. He showed himself in this way so that he could reveal the true nature of God.

In one of the most evident displays of servanthood, Jesus stooped to one of the lowest means of serving; so low, in fact, that Peter initially refused to allow it to happen:

> *...so he got up from the meal, took off his outer clothing, and wrapped a towel around his waist. After that, he poured water into a basin and began to wash*

his disciples' feet, drying them with the towel that was
wrapped around him.[3]

Now that is serving! Imagine the dirt and dust that would have collected on these men's feet. But, in an effort to show his love for his disciples, and ultimately for us, Jesus stooped down to wash their feet. Do you think Jesus felt like he was belittling himself? Do you believe Jesus saw this as a chore or an opportunity?

In order to become more like Christ, we must not consider ourselves above anyone, especially our spouse. Instead, the opposite is true. We should be searching for ways to serve our spouse. As Peter said in his first letter, we are called to "love deeply" and to use the gifts we have been given to serve others.

Personalize Your Serving

There's no formula for becoming a servant in your marriage. Each marriage relationship is different as each man and woman is different. Not every woman wants her husband in the kitchen – I can recall more than one time when Anne has actually banned me from entering the kitchen! In the same way, there are men out there who prefer to handle all the landscaping and other yard work without the help of their wives.

You know your husband or wife better than anyone on the planet. You should be able to list off at least ten areas where you could serve in your marriage. And if you can't, then ask. Find out where you can serve best. Is there a physical need? Does your spouse need encouragement? Are there tasks on a to-do list that you could take over?

In the same way, each of us is blessed with certain gifts when it comes to serving. 1 Peter 4:10 says, "Each one should use whatever gift he has received to serve others, faithfully administering God's grace in its various forms."[4]

Some of us are more apt to physical serving – taking on more chores, helping out with the kids, washing the car – while others are more effective in encouraging or praying. No matter where your strengths may lie, start serving your spouse in that capacity.

However, we can't be limited to only serving in areas where we feel comfortable or have experience. If your spouse is in need of prayer and spiritual support, don't back away just because you're more of a physical servant. Open your heart to both your spouse and to God, and you will be amazed at the transformation in your marriage.

The Effects of Serving

John Ortberg presented another powerful message in *The Life You've Always Wanted*. He said, "The primary reason Jesus calls us to serve is not just because other people need our service. It is because of what happens to us when we serve."[5]

Yes, it's possible that our spouse could make it through the day without our service. But, when we make an effort to serve, when we truly reach out to help when there's a need, not only is our spouse better off, but we are also.

Almost every morning, I am the first one awake in the house. I sometimes start my day an hour or so before Anne or the kids even begin to stir. As often as I can remember, just before waking Anne, I go downstairs to make her coffee. After adding a little coffee to her flavored creamer, I head up the stairs to wake my wife with the proud news that her coffee is waiting.

Anne loves her morning coffee. Sometimes she will take that first sip, close her eyes and moan a little sound of pure bliss. It really does make her happy. (It's like those coffee

54

commercials, only it's my wife and she's not quite as bright-eyed after that first sip.) And, she appreciates my efforts to make her coffee.

I don't drink coffee. It's not that I'm making it for myself, and, oh by the way, I made an extra cup for you, too. Making Anne's coffee is a deliberate act of service to her. It's just a little act of service, but it makes all the difference in a morning. And, do you know what else? I feel good when I see her enjoying her coffee. I feel good when she tells me, "Thanks," and gives me my first hug and kiss of the day. It feels good when she says, "You're the best husband in the world." All that for a little cup of coffee! Anne is happy and gets her morning started off right. I'm feeling good because I know she's happy.

Taking It for Granted

On the other hand, there are times when I forget to make the coffee or I'm too rushed in the morning to make the trip downstairs before kicking Anne out of bed. Just like every other morning, though, she needs her coffee. Although it's not meant to be expected, it kind of is, and Anne's not herself when her coffee isn't ready. I feel bad that I forgot or chose not to make it that morning. All in all, the morning just doesn't get off to a good start.

In this instance, there was nothing deliberately hurtful on either Anne's or my part, but rather the circumstances just lead to a different result. However, it can become intentional. We can get used to the servant treatment we receive from our spouse. If your wife is great at serving – in the kitchen, with the kids, around the house – you might get used to that. After all, there is that great feeling we get when we serve, right? We would hate to keep her from that feeling.

But, if you are not doing a thing to serve her, there isn't a balance. There's too much serving on one side of the marriage and not enough on the other. Instead, we need to get off our rears and start doing something before "serving joyfully" becomes "serving painfully," and that's not the servant's heart we're looking for.

In the same way, if one spouse feels like he or she is always doing more of the serving, there is a tendency for that spouse to feel like he or she *deserves* to be served more by the other. This also serves as a recipe for disaster.

I see this more in wives than husbands, but it can certainly go either way. Many wives, by nature, take on a great deal. A wife's list of responsibilities just seems to be naturally longer than her husband's. And much of that list includes things that would most certainly fall into the "serving" category: cooking, cleaning, bathing the kids, shopping, folding, and planning. Often times, when all these things add up, the balance of who is serving who and how much does seem to be out of whack.

But the moment that we begin to keep score and measure service against service, we nullify the whole meaning of serving like Christ served. Do you think Christ kept a tally sheet of how many people he healed, expecting that the favor would be returned some day? After washing the disciple's feet, did Jesus say, "Okay. Now you do me."? No. He said:

> *"Do you understand what I have done for you?" he asked them. "You call me 'Teacher' and 'Lord,' and rightly so, for that is what I am. Now that I, your Lord and Teacher, have washed your feet, you also should wash one another's feet. I have set you an example that you should do as I have done for you. I tell you the truth, no servant is greater than his master, nor is a messenger greater than the one who sent him. Now*

that you know these things, you will be blessed if you
do them.''[6]

Nowhere in there does Jesus say that we are to keep score. Instead, he says we are to follow his example and wash each other's feet. We should serve our spouse because we want to, not because we feel we have to, or in order that we might point out the fact later and say, "Remember, I did this for you, so you should do this for me."

When we truly love and serve our spouse like Jesus loved and served his disciples, the result will be a servant's heart striving to become more like Christ. You can't control how he or she will respond in turn; only God has that power. And, when God is working in your marriage, his power will be manifested through changed lives in both you and your spouse.

From the Chapter

"In order to become more like Christ, we must not consider ourselves above anyone, especially our spouse. Instead, the opposite is true. We should be searching for ways to serve our spouse."

Bible Verse Reference

Mark 10:45 – "For even the Son of Man did not come to be served, but to serve, and to give his life as a ransom for many."

Question:

List seven things that you can do to serve your spouse this week. Find one area to serve each day, and then resolve to do it.

Chapter 5

Honesty is the Best Policy

"If we claim to be without sin, we deceive ourselves and the truth is not in us." (I John 1:8)

In the movie *Liar, Liar*, Jim Carey plays the role of Fletcher Reede, a lawyer and dad who never keeps the promises he makes to his son. On his birthday, Fletcher's son makes a birthday wish that his dad couldn't tell a lie for one whole day. When that wish comes true, Fletcher has quite a time making it through his day.

At one point, he walks into his office where he's confronted by a young secretary with a bit of a goofy appearance and matching personality who proudly displays her new, loud plaid dress.

"Hi, Mr. Reede. Like my new dress?" she says with excitement.

Fletcher's truthful response: "Whatever takes the focus off your head!"[1]

Now, that's honesty! But, is that the kind of honesty that will strengthen a marriage? Is that the kind of honesty Jesus displayed in his life? Most definitely not. Then what does it mean to have a marriage that's based on complete honesty?

Brutal vs. Complete

Two thoughts come to mind when I think of honesty in this context. One is shown by Fletcher in the example above. But, there is a difference between brutal honesty and complete honesty. In his letter to the Ephesians, Paul writes:

> *Do not let any unwholesome talk come out of your mouths, but only what is helpful for building others up according to their needs, that it may benefit those who listen.[2]*

Being honest with our spouse involves sharing sincere opinions, providing truthful input and offering straightforward advice. It does not mean we have to point out every flaw or comment on every outfit. Paul says we should be "building up others according to their needs." When we blurt out the first thing that comes to mind or even put some thought into a comment that, although true, could be hurtful, we are displaying what Paul called "unwholesome talk."

If our goal is to build up our spouse with our words, we must make a conscious effort to do so. Even in a relationship where sarcasm is accepted, or even encouraged, a harsh – albeit truthful – word can do a good deal of damage. In fact, sometimes we should just hold our tongues. In his book *Life Together*, Dietrich Bonhoeffer said:

> *Often we combat our evil thoughts most effectively if we absolutely refuse to allow them to be expressed in words...It must be a decisive rule of every Christian fellowship that each individual is prohibited from saying much that occurs to him.*[3]

We are constantly faced with instances where the first thing that comes to mind is probably not the first thing that should be said. While this doesn't mean that we should make something up just to be nice, it does mean that we should think a little bit longer about how we might be able to phrase our response in a kinder manner. Proverbs 15:23 says, "...how good is a timely word!"[4] If we can build up, while at the same time being honest and sincere in our words, how positive that will be in our marriage.

No Secrets

The second thought around this concept of honesty in marriage involves keeping no secrets from your spouse. Your husband or wife should be the one person that knows everything about you. If there are areas in our lives that are hidden, we need to examine those areas and discover why they are hidden. In most cases, I believe we hide certain things because we are embarrassed about some habit or we flat out know that if our spouse knew about it, there would be a negative or possibly severe response.

I speak from experience in this particular matter. From the time we met, I had a secret that I held from Anne. I had kept this one area of my life hidden from everyone for a long time, and even though I promised to share everything with her, I couldn't let go of this one thing.

The summer before I entered the seventh grade, I was molested by a young man in our church. At the young age of twelve, I was thrust into a world I had no idea existed. Along with the biological timing of things already taking place in my body as an adolescent boy, this experience exposed sexual feelings and curiosity I didn't know what to do with.

What started as a minor interest in department store catalogs, over the course of several years turned into an exploration of magazines and nudity in movies. When I reached college, my newfound freedom lead to a more frequent involvement with pornography. Then, with the advent of the Internet and its ability to offer sexually explicit web sites to just about anyone at any time, I became addicted and struggled with this area of my life on a daily basis.

This is a brief bird's eye view covering a span of 20 years of dealing with this secret area of my life, twelve of which involved time when I was either dating or married to Anne. I was ashamed. I was embarrassed. I knew what I was doing was wrong, but I couldn't bear to tell Anne about my struggles. What would she think? What would she do? How would she respond? So, I kept it hidden away.

Confession

Hopefully, you can take this story and learn from it and realize never to keep anything from your spouse. Addressing a situation after the fact creates a strain in your marriage that is not easily overcome. But, if you're like many of the people I have shared this story with, you already have your own hidden area in your life, and now you need to deal with it.

The first thing we must do is to release this hidden area to God. For 20 years I had tried to fight this battle by myself, and I knew that had to change. I John 1:9 says, "If we confess our sins, he is faithful and just and will forgive us our sins and purify us from all unrighteousness."[5] We cannot do it on our own. Only with Christ's help can we truly be released from the bondage of sin.

After releasing the situation to God, the next thing we must do is confess to our spouse, the person we have sinned against. It doesn't matter if you're keeping a secret that involves pornography or gambling or alcohol or drugs or cigarettes or chewing tobacco, or even friendships that have gone too far or work issues that you've hidden from your spouse. You must open yourself up to your spouse and be completely honest about this hidden area of your life.

In *The Life You've Always Wanted*, John Ortberg said it this way:

> *Confession means saying that somewhere in the mix was a choice, and the choice was made by us, and it*

> *does not need to be excused, explained or even*
> *understood. The choice needs to be forgiven. The slate*
> *has to be wiped clean.*[6]

I had confessed to God and had been free of my addiction for over a year, but it was during the preparations for a mission trip to Mexico that the Lord really showed me that I needed to confess to Anne. I knew before then that I had to tell her at some point, but until I put it completely into God's hands, I always had an excuse for not saying anything.

(The order in which you take these steps of confession is important. To truly be moving in the direction of reconciliation, you must first confess to God and ask for his forgiveness. And you must have faith that Christ will work in you to address whatever it is you are keeping from your spouse. Then, you should confess to your spouse with the full intent of addressing this area, with God's help and with the help of your spouse.)

When I returned from Mexico, I told Anne everything. I didn't know of any other way to do it than to just be honest and open about this addiction that had crippled me for so long. I shared with her how that experience as a child had progressed into a problem that I could not control. I told her how the Lord had been working in me for so long, and yet how stubborn and selfish I had been all this time. I felt a tremendous weight lifted off of my back, a weight that had held me down for so long.

And, yet, now there was a different weight. Even in my confession, there was a certain degree of selfishness. While it felt so good to be getting all of this off my chest and finally opening up and confessing this to my wife, I was dumping a load of unbelievable weight onto her. That's the flip side of confession. When you finally get up the courage to confess to your spouse, you must be prepared for the repercussions; and it's not always going to be an arms open wide, "I'm glad you told me, now let's get on with our lives" type of response.

I'm not going to sugar-coat it. That was the worst week of my life. For so long, I had lied to her. I had hidden something from her. I had pretended to be something I wasn't. I was hypocritical. With every right, Anne felt betrayed. How could she trust me? How sad did this make her feel? She was disappointed. She was angry. She was hurt.

John Ortberg said, "True confession involves entering into the pain of the person we have hurt and entering into God's pain over sin."[7] At this point, I finally realized what I had done. I realized the pain I had caused by my selfish actions. I realized that Anne deserved better than this. And I knew there was only one thing that would keep us together: Forgiveness. (We'll talk more about this in the next chapter.)

Being Honest with Yourself

Once you confess, that's not the end. John Ortberg said:

> *When we practice confession well, two things happen. The first is that we are liberated from guilt. The second is that we will be at least a little less likely to sin in the same way in the future than if we had not confessed. Sin will look and feel less attractive…Confession is not just naming what we have done in the past. It involves our intentions about the future as well. It requires a kind of promise…We resolve that, with God's help, we will change.*[8]

This is where the power of the Holy Spirit becomes the strength we can depend on. Notice how Ortberg says here, "with God's help…" It is not by our own power that we confess and then change, but only with God's help. It's not natural to want to confess and open ourselves up to possible ridicule and

68

shame. It's much easier to keep something hidden. We tell ourselves, "No one will ever find out. I just won't do it again, and everything will be okay."

But we must be honest with ourselves. We must first be honest with God, then be honest with our spouse, and then resolve to be honest with ourselves about what we have confessed. When we are honest in every part of our marriage, we are conforming to the likeness of Jesus.

From the Chapter

"Your husband or wife should be the one person that knows everything about you. If there are areas in our lives that are hidden, we need to examine those areas and discover why they are hidden."

Bible Verse Reference

1 John 1:9 – "If we confess our sins, he is faithful and just and will forgive us our sins and purify us from all unrighteousness."

Question:

Are there areas in your life that you are hiding from your spouse? Pray for the courage to open up to your spouse and become completely honest with him or her. Then, ask for forgiveness.

Chapter 6

Forgiveness is Key

"For if you forgive men when they sin against you, your heavenly
Father will also forgive you."
(Matthew 6:14)

One Bible story that stuck with me ever since I was a kid is the story about Peter asking Jesus how many times he should forgive someone who has sinned against him. Jesus first replies with what would seem to be an absurd number of times – "seventy times seven"[1] – and then he follows with a parable about forgiveness.

Although *The Message* Bible did not exist when I was young, I like how this story reads in its translation:

> *At that point Peter got up the nerve to ask, "Master, how many times do I forgive a brother or sister who hurts me? Seven?"*
>
> *Jesus replied, "Seven! Hardly. Try seventy times seven.*

"The kingdom of God is like a king who decided to square accounts with his servants. As he got under way, one servant was brought before him who had run up a debt of a hundred thousand dollars. He couldn't pay up, so the king ordered the man, along with his wife, children, and goods, to be auctioned off at the slave market.

"The poor wretch threw himself at the king's feet and begged, 'Give me a chance and I'll pay it all back.' Touched by his plea, the king let him off, erasing the debt.

"The servant was no sooner out of the room when he came upon one of his fellow servants who owed him ten dollars. He seized him by the throat and demanded, 'Pay up. Now!'

"The poor wretch threw himself down and begged, 'Give me a chance and I'll pay it all back.' But he wouldn't do it. He had him arrested and put in jail until the debt was paid. When the other servants saw this

*going on, they were outraged and brought a detailed
report to the king.*

*"The king summoned the man and said, 'You evil
servant! I forgave your entire debt when you begged
me for mercy. Shouldn't you be compelled to be
merciful to your fellow servant who asked for mercy?'
The king was furious and put the screws to the man
until he paid back his entire debt. And that's exactly
what my Father in heaven is going to do to each one of
you who doesn't forgive unconditionally anyone who
asks for mercy."[2]*

Hearing this story as a child, I thought, "Man, 490 times?
That's a lot of forgiving!" But, that's the point, isn't it? We are
to never stop forgiving. And Jesus makes the point very clear
that unless we forgive others, our Father in heaven will not
forgive us.

*For if you forgive men when they sin against you, your
heavenly Father will also forgive you. But if you do not*

forgive men their sins, your Father will not forgive your sins.[3]

And when you stand praying, if you hold anything against anyone, forgive him, so that your Father in heaven may forgive you your sins.[4]

Forgiveness: Essential to Marriage

You hear about it all the time, husbands and wives working through difficulties in their marriage. Whether it is a problem of money, lying, or any other issue, even a betrayal as great as adultery, when couples are committed to a long-term marriage, forgiveness is essential. We all make mistakes, and without true forgiveness offered to or received from our spouse, those mistakes will add up to a debt that none of us can ever repay.

Even at a time when forgiveness would be the last thing on any of our minds, Jesus said, as he hung on the cross, "Father, forgive them, for they do not know what they are doing."[5] As we strive to be like Christ in our marriage, how can we *not* forgive our spouse for whatever he or she has done? Is it an offense worse than murder? Jesus forgave the people who were killing him!

The same story from earlier in the chapter as written in the New International Version says that Jesus replied, "I tell you, not seven times, but seventy times seven." We are called to forgive and forgive and forgive. That's living a life like Jesus.

Have you ever gone to bed with something left unsettled? Either you need to ask for forgiveness from your spouse, or maybe you need to offer it? I often find myself thinking very selfishly in these instances. I think, "I didn't do anything wrong. I don't need to ask for forgiveness." Or, "I can't believe she said that. How could she have said that? She didn't even say she was sorry!" And then I think, as I lay there *not* falling asleep, about what I should have done or said in response or how I'll react the next time that situation comes up again.

And then something happens. Over the next few days, I start to get eaten up from inside. I begin to harbor resentment over something that was said. It boils up inside me. I start to relate it to other things going on, and it comes across in my attitude toward Anne and the kids. All this because I didn't think I did anything wrong!

We need to humble ourselves before God and before our spouse. In order to be forgiven, we must forgive. And, in order to be forgiven, we must ask for forgiveness.

A friend of ours suggested a little tool to help instill the idea of forgiveness to our kids. I think the same concept applies to married couples. It's not enough just to say, "I'm sorry." We should take it a step further and say, "I'm sorry. Will you forgive me?" It takes the understanding of the situation to a whole other level. By asking for forgiveness, you are admitting that there is a need to be forgiven.

And, if we are the forgiver, we need to become more like Jesus as he said we must "forgive unconditionally anyone who asks for mercy."

Forgiving Others

Many times, forgiveness involves a situation outside of the marriage relationship and yet still causes issues within the marriage that need to be resolved through forgiveness. It might be a friend of your wife who said something rude about you. It may be a situation at work that's been bothering you and keeps you up at night, therefore causing stress inside the marriage. It could be any number of external issues where there is a need for forgiveness to enter into the situation – whether asking for forgiveness or offering it to someone else – in order to help get your marriage back on track.

I skipped one vital element in the last chapter regarding my own confession. In addition to confessing to God and confessing to Anne and asking her to forgive me, I had to forgive the person who had hurt me so long ago. For years, I had blamed the man who had molested me for my own sexual immorality. I told myself it was his fault I was involved in pornography, and it was him who had pushed me into this addiction that was affecting me in so many ways. Often times, we put this same blame on our spouse – "if he/she wouldn't have done _____ (fill in the blank), then I wouldn't be doing _____ (fill in the blank)." We must realize, though, that it's our own behavior, not theirs, that truly causes us to stumble.

For so long, I had tried to forgive him. Many times I had even prayed a prayer of forgiveness *toward* him. But, there was still something that wouldn't allow me to completely let go. Every time I read about forgiveness in the Bible or heard a sermon preached that addressed the subject of forgiveness, I thought of this man. I knew I had to go further than offering forgiveness "toward" him; I had to offer forgiveness "to" him.

Forgiveness, I found, is such a powerful tool given to us by God. The verses mentioned above in Matthew 6:14-15, kept hitting me. "For if you forgive men when they sin against you,

77

your heavenly Father will also forgive you. But if you do not forgive men their sins, your Father will not forgive your sins."

So, I did. I made contact with him and forgave him. I also asked for his forgiveness for harboring so much hate for so long and for blaming him for all of my own sins. And, once I offered genuine forgiveness to this person, I was forgiven myself. What a wonderful feeling that is! I became liberated and experienced a freedom I had not felt in 20 years. You have heard stories of crack junkies turning from an uncontrollable addiction to an incomprehensible freedom overnight. This was my story. I was a completely changed man.

In my case, this was the second step in my process of confessing and changing my life. I realized I had to confess to God; I had to offer forgiveness to the person who I blamed for all these years; and then I had to confess to Anne and ask for her forgiveness.

Forgiveness, not Forget-ness

Forgiveness does not mean "forget-ness." Being forgiven does not mean that your spouse will just forget about whatever it was that required the act of forgiving. Depending on the situation, it may require a time of healing, a time of rebuilding that trust you once had.

Rick Warren said,

> *Many people are reluctant to show mercy because they don't understand the difference between trust and forgiveness. Forgiveness is letting go of the past. Trust has to do with future behavior.*

> *Forgiveness must be immediate, whether or not a person asks for it. Trust must be rebuilt over time. Trust requires a track record. If someone hurts you repeatedly, you are commanded by God to forgive them instantly, but you are not expected to trust them immediately, and you are not expected to continue allowing them to hurt you.[6]*

And, once we have truly offered forgiveness, we cannot continue to bring up "that time when…" years from now when it suits a particular purpose. That goes totally against Jesus' point of "seventy times seven." We are told to simply forgive, as many times as it takes. Just remember, God has forgiven you more times than you will ever have the opportunity to forgive someone else.

From the Chapter

"As we strive to be like Christ in our marriage, how can we *not* forgive our spouse for whatever he or she has done? Is it an offense worse than murder? Jesus forgave the people who were killing him!"

Bible Verse Reference

Mark 11:25 – "And when you stand praying, if you hold anything against anyone, forgive him, so that your Father in heaven may forgive you your sins."

Question:

Do you need to ask for forgiveness from your spouse? Are you the one who should be offering forgiveness? Do it today, and do it with sincerity.

Chapter 7

Humble Yourself

"Do not think of yourself more highly than you ought, but rather think of yourself with sober judgment, in accordance with the measure of faith God has given you."
(Romans 12:3)

There's a television commercial running now for a certain brand of car. The car maker is creatively pointing out why people drive such fancy cars. One driver of an elegant sedan is announcing out his window using a bull horn, "Because Daddy never hugged me. Because Daddy never hugged me." While another in a high-end sports car cries out, "Because I have more money than you. Because I have more money than you." In the end, the humble driver of the mid-level brand car tosses her bull horn out the window, as if to say, "I don't need to announce why I have this car. It's just a good car."

That's really how life is, isn't it? Whether it's just dealing with people on a daily basis who tend to place themselves a little higher than everyone else, or it might be that your sister claims more significance than you because of her status in life.

81

We have to face it every day. But Christ, the only one who actually had every right to be prideful and arrogant, chose to humble himself.

> *Your attitude should be the same as that of Christ Jesus: Who, being in very nature God, did not consider equality with God something to be grasped, but made himself nothing, taking the very nature of a servant, being made in human likeness. And being found in appearance as a man, he humbled himself and became obedient to death—even death on a cross!*[1]

Self-Forgetfulness

John Ortberg, in *The Life You've Always Wanted*, said, "Humility has to do with submitted willingness. It involves a healthy self-forgetfulness."[2] In marriage, that is key! "Self-forgetfulness" is quite possibly the most valuable word in marriage. And, at the same time, it is indeed one of the most difficult to implement.

I just had a conversation with someone the other day about this very topic. Our discussion was focused on putting our wives ahead of ourselves. Our struggle ultimately came down to the fact that we both think we're pretty darn good husbands! Compared to our dads and other dads out there, we help much more around the house; we are more hands-on with the kids; we do a lot to serve our wives.

As I'm sure you can see where this is going, we were pretty high on ourselves. We even got to the point of saying, "Why don't they recognize how great we are?" Are we selfish or what? The reality of it is, there's nothing special about what we're doing as husbands and fathers. We're called to serve our wives and to be good parents. We shouldn't expect credit when we do a good job at it. And, we certainly shouldn't be comparing ourselves to anyone else and the good or bad job they may be doing.

When a marriage consists of a husband and wife whose ultimate goal is to do whatever it takes to please God and please each other, that marriage will succeed. Self plays no role in that equation. John Ortberg describes:

> *At the deepest level, pride is the choice to exclude both God and other people from their rightful place in our hearts. Jesus said that the essence of spiritual life is to*

> *love God and love people. Pride destroys our capacity*
> *to love...pride is a form of antilove.*[3]

Headship without Pride

God describes this ideal marriage relationship in Ephesians.
We've already reviewed this in Chapter 1:

> *Submit to one another out of reverence for Christ.*
> *Wives, submit to your husbands as to the Lord. For the*
> *husband is the head of the wife as Christ is the head of*
> *the church, his body, of which he is the Savior. Now as*
> *the church submits to Christ, so also wives should*
> *submit to their husbands in everything. Husbands, love*
> *your wives, just as Christ loved the church and gave*
> *himself up for her to make her holy, cleansing her by*
> *the washing with water through the word, and to*
> *present her to himself as a radiant church, without*
> *stain or wrinkle or any other blemish, but holy and*
> *blameless. In this same way, husbands ought to love*
> *their wives as their own bodies. He who loves his wife*
> *loves himself. After all, no one ever hated his own*
> *body, but he feeds and cares for it, just as Christ does*

> *the church— for we are members of his body. For this*
> *reason a man will leave his father and mother and be*
> *united to his wife, and the two will become one flesh.*
> *This is a profound mystery—but I am talking about*
> *Christ and the church. However, each one of you also*
> *must love his wife as he loves himself, and the wife*
> *must respect her husband.[4]*

For those of you who have been waiting to get to that
"submit" word, here we go! However, you might be surprised
as you go back and re-read the verses above. The first verse
says, "Submit *to one another* out of reverence for Christ."

I'll admit it; I never read this verse with regard to the rest
of this passage. It always starts with the next verse, "Wives,
submit…" I have always looked past this one, probably because
it's just above the header in my study Bible! But, in fact,
husbands and wives are to submit to each other out of reverence
for Christ. This verse then leads into the ways in which we
should humble ourselves in this way. I'll start with the
husbands.

"For the husband is the head of the wife as Christ is the
head of the church, his body, of which he is the

85

Savior...Husbands, love your wives, just as Christ loved the church...husbands ought to love their wives as their own bodies. He who loves his wife loves himself."

Husbands, our role as head of the wife is compared to Christ's role as head of the church. This is not a picture of a dictator or dominator, but rather the image of a head in its relation to the rest of the body. What is good for the head is good for the whole body. Christ is one with the church and loves the church so much that he is determined to make it all that it should be.

The true head who loves and is one with his wife will never embitter her or dominate her. That's completely contrary to the ideal relationship as exemplified between Christ and the church. There is no pride associated with fulfilling our role as head of our wives.

Submit is Not a Four-Letter Word

"Wives, submit to your husbands as to the Lord...Now as the church submits to Christ, so also wives should submit to their husbands in everything...and the wife must respect her husband."

In light of the role defined above of the husband as the head, submission, then, is not a negative, but a positive result of confidence in the unity and love of the head with the body. Submission for the wife means that she willingly acknowledges the headship of her husband over her, and has confidence in God that he has set this authority over her for her own good.[5]

This concept is addressed by Paul in Romans 12:3-5:

> *Do not think of yourself more highly than you ought, but rather think of yourself with sober judgment, in accordance with the measure of faith God has given you. Just as each of us has one body with many members, and these members do not all have the same function, so in Christ we who are many form one body, and each member belongs to all the others.[6]*

As a married couple, we form one body in Christ. The husband is designated as the head, to lead and direct the wife as the body. But, a head cannot survive without its body; and the body will not make it far without a head. There is no pride in either function. "If one part suffers, every part suffers with it; if one part is honored, every part rejoices with it."[7]

87

Do Show Pride for Your Spouse

We all have moments of positive pride. When our infant takes his first steps. When our company wins a big new piece of business. When the Cavaliers beat the Pistons! In this way, we are instructed to take pride in our spouse as well. Christ is proud of his bride, as Paul describes how Christ will "present her to himself as a radiant church, without stain or wrinkle or any other blemish, but holy and blameless."

A loving husband will be able to present to himself his wife in all her glory, set apart for him, perfect in her womanhood. After many years of marriage, she will be a woman at peace, a woman who responds lovingly to him in every way. And it will be apparent to all that this man is a man of love.

A wife who submits and loves and respects her husband will enjoy the benefits of a secure and loving marriage relationship. She will be proud of her husband who loves and cares for her like Christ does his church.[8]

This is definitely something to be proud of – a humble relationship molded after the life of Jesus Christ.

From the Chapter

"When a marriage consists of a husband and wife whose ultimate goal is to do whatever it takes to please God and please each other, that marriage will succeed."

Bible Verse Reference

Philippians 2:5-7 – "Your attitude should be the same as that of Christ Jesus: Who, being in very nature God, did not consider equality with God something to be grasped, but made himself nothing, taking the very nature of a servant, being made in human likeness."

Question:

In what area of your life do you struggle most with pride? What steps can you take to eliminate that pride?

Chapter 8

One Flesh

"'For this reason a man shall leave his father and mother and be united to his wife, and the two will become one flesh.' So they are no longer two, but one. Therefore, what God has joined together, let man not separate" (Mark 10:7-9)

Have you ever caught yourself in a daze looking out the window when it's raining? Or watching the water drip down the glass door of the shower? Or even anticipating the condensation as it gathers on a glass of iced tea? I find myself sometimes in awe as one droplet moves down a particular path until it combines with another droplet and the two then move together as one down the glass.

This is how I envision God's description of the relationship of husband and wife in Genesis 2:24. "For this reason a man shall leave his father and mother and be united with his wife, *and they will become one flesh.*"[1] Becoming one flesh is like those two droplets flowing together to make the journey as one for the rest of their existence. Once they meet in the flow, there is no distinguishing one from the other. There is no separation. One is not stronger or better or more impressive than the other.

To take this analogy further, when those two drops form one, the new drop is bigger and more powerful than the two were separately, isn't it? The same is true for a husband and wife who truly implement the idea of one flesh into their lives. They become a great force when they are bound together in Christ; a strong force that is extremely difficult to divide.

Always One

Can you remember a special gift you received when you were a child? Was there one special present that you had to have? I remember getting an electric race car track when I was about eight years old. It was one that had two cars that were controlled separately by hand-held triggers. I got it for Christmas that year, and for several weeks no one could tear me away from my new race car set. Any free time I had was spent playing with it. You could almost say I was "one" with this toy.

But, after a few weeks, you can guess what happened. As I'm sure you have a similar story, something better came along, and I played with the race car set less and less. Like many things in our lives, that toy became a temporary obsession that received a lot of my attention. In God's eyes, marriage is not one of those things. The unity between husband and wife, like that of Christ and the church, is not something that happens occasionally, or even regularly; the two are essentially one at all times.[2]

Paul emphasizes this when he says "husbands ought to love their wives as their own bodies. He who loves his wife loves himself. After all, no one ever hated his own body, but he feeds and cares for it, just as Christ does the church...each one of you also must love his wife as he loves himself"[3]

We take care of our bodies so we stay healthy. We can't just eat right sometimes and expect to feel good and stay at a healthy weight. We have to be consistent in our patterns of healthy eating and exercise. A healthy marriage works the same way. We can't love and nourish our spouse one day, and then decide not to the next day. And we can't be close with and love our spouse only when it's easy or beneficial for us. We must consider ourselves one with our spouse all the time.

In Perfect Harmony

When you think of a couple who exemplifies the concept of unity in their marriage, who comes to mind? There's probably at least one couple that you can think of who fits the definition perfectly – they finish each other's sentences; they teach a Sunday School class together; they always seem to get along wonderfully.

Anne and I were friends with a couple when we lived in South Carolina, and they were this perfect couple. I've run into a few others that display these characteristics of harmony and unity, but these two really seemed to have it all together. You can tell when it's just for show or if they truly are unified with a purpose and foundation in Christ.

While it's great to witness and learn from people you may know, the true perfect example of unity is represented in the Trinity of God the Father, God the Son and God the Holy Spirit. This unified body of three-in-one provides us with a view of how unity really works. In fact, we were created in the image of God – Father, Son and Spirit.

> *'Let us make man in our image, in our likeness...' So God created man in his own image, in the image of God he created him...*[4]

So, at our core, we are united as the Trinity is united, and thus we should be united as one with our spouse, as God has commanded.

The three persons of the Trinity work together, in partnership, with one goal in mind – to save the world which is lost. First, God the Father created the heavens and the Earth, and he created man to rule over the earth. God then sent his only son to be humbled and live life as a man on this planet, and ultimately to die on a cross to save us from our sins. Then, the Holy Spirit came upon the early Christians in the same way he washes over us today. The three persons are working in sync to accomplish a single mission.

Can you image if the Trinity somehow miscommunicated with each other? What if the Holy Spirit decided to come first? There would have been some awfully confused people. What if God said, "I'm not ready. Holy Spirit and Jesus, you guys start this thing off, and I'll follow your lead." Luckily, that wasn't the case. God the Father, Son and Holy Spirit are in perfect harmony and are playing out the perfect plan.

Unity on All Fronts

Unity doesn't just apply to the marriage relationship itself. If you have children, you know that one of the most difficult areas for unity is related to raising those children. Our pastor and his wife call it a "unified front" when they discuss being on the same page with your spouse regarding discipline, in particular.

One of the worst things that can happen between a parent and child is for the child to recognize opportunities to pit one parent against the other. If we have a unified front across the board, the likelihood for such a situation to occur is much, much less. If we are not unified, this gives rise to arguments, misunderstandings and frustrations between you and your spouse about even the little decisions in parenting.

Besides parenting, we also need to be united in our finances, our social circles and our spiritual walks. In every area of our lives, being united with our spouse will allow for growth as individuals, as a couple, and as a family.

Paul says to the Corinthians:

> *I appeal to you, brothers, in the name of our Lord Jesus Christ, that all of you agree with one another so that there may be no divisions among you and that you may be perfectly united in mind and thought.*[5]

If we are perfectly united in mind and thought with our spouse, can you imagine the strength of that relationship?

Psalm 133:1 says, "How good and pleasant it is when brothers live together in unity!"[6]

From the Chapter

"We can't love and nourish our spouse one day, and then decide not to the next day. And we can't be close with and love our spouse only when it's easy or beneficial for us. We must consider ourselves one with our spouse all the time."

Bible Verse Reference

1 Corinthians 1:10 – "I appeal to you, brothers, in the name of our Lord Jesus Christ, that all of you agree with one another so that there may be no divisions among you and that you may be perfectly united in mind and thought."

Question:

Would you consider you and your spouse to be "one flesh?" What one thing can you do today to become closer to your spouse than you are right now?

Chapter 9

Faithful in Prayer

"Be joyful in hope, patient in affliction, faithful in prayer."
(Romans 12:12)

One of my earliest memories of my dad is one that has stuck with me vividly for all these years. What seemed to be without fail, every morning my dad would go into his closet and pray. I would always know he was in there because the light would be on, even when I went into my parent's bedroom after waking up very early as a young child, sometimes at four or five o'clock on the morning.

There were two things I knew about my dad's time in his closet: 1) we were never allowed to disturb him; and 2) it was a very special time for him.

I don't know when he started his daily prayer sessions or really for how long he prayed when he did, but at times it seemed like he was in there for hours. Occasionally he would mention that I was on his prayer list or that someone I knew was on the list. I just couldn't imagine what he could be doing in there for so long every single day.

Now, as a husband, father, employee, deacon, friend and brother, I realize the need for continuous prayer. My marriage needs prayer. My children need prayer. Our church needs prayer. My friends need prayer. Our leaders need prayer. Our teachers, our children's friends, our brothers and sisters, our small group, our babysitter...and the list goes on.

Prayer is essential to developing a life like Christ. Jesus even goes so far as to teach us exactly how we should pray.

> *This then is how you should pray: 'Our Father in heaven, hallowed be your name, your kingdom come, your will be done on earth as it is in heaven. Give us this day our daily bread. Forgive us our debts, as we also have forgiven our debtors. And lead us not into temptation, but deliver us from the evil one.'[1]*

The Bible says that we are to pray for those who persecute us, pray so that we don't fall into temptation, pray continually, pray with joy, pray for help, pray for each other. Jesus puts a strong emphasis on prayer, and he leads with a very strong example.

Jesus and Prayer

Just before Jesus gave us what is commonly known as The Lord's Prayer mentioned above, he gave some stern warnings about our attitude when we pray:

> *And when you pray, do not be like the hypocrites, for they love to pray standing in the synagogues and on the street corners to be seen by men. I tell you the truth, they have received their reward in full. But when you pray, go into your room, close the door and pray to your Father, who is unseen. Then your Father, who sees what is done in secret, will reward you. And when you pray, do not keep on babbling like pagans, for they think they will be heard because of their many words. Do not be like them, for your Father knows what you need before you ask him.[2]*

Several times the Bible records Jesus praying in a quite place alone. "Very early in the morning, while it was still dark, Jesus got up, left the house and went off to a solitary place, where he prayed."[3]

When he was in the garden of Gethsemane on the night he was betrayed, Jesus had left his disciples so that he could be alone to pray. Matthew 26:39 says, "Going a little farther, he fell with his face to the ground and prayed,"[4] and in one of the most desperate prayers recorded in the Bible, Jesus prays that God will not allow what is about to happen to him.

When Jesus prayed, he prayed with focus, with determination, with intention. And when it came down to the most important circumstances of his life, he prayed alone in a quite place. To be like Jesus, we need to follow his example.

Not for Show

Praying is not for show. God wants us to focus on him when we are talking with him through prayer. In *Purpose Driven Life*, Rick Warren says:

> *God is not pleased with thoughtless singing of hymns, perfunctory praying of clichés, or careless exclamations of "Praise the Lord," because we can't think of anything else to say at that moment. If worship is mindless, it is meaningless. You must engage your mind.*[5]

Recently, my son, Isaac, has been resisting me when it comes time for him to pray before bedtime. I'll usually start by praying out loud to thank God for the day, to ask him to watch over Isaac as he goes to sleep, to protect him all through the night, and to ask for a good tomorrow. Then, when it's his turn, Isaac will say, "I just prayed in my head." Even though it's possible he did pray in his head, I have tried to talk with him about how Jesus likes to "hear" him.

Now, I know it's not necessary to speak out loud in order for God to hear our prayers. But, if you take the mindset of a four-year-old and apply it to our situation as adults, there are some similarities. In reality, my guess is that he didn't say the prayer in his head, which means he's not really focusing on his prayer time with God. I am often the same way. I try to get my prayer time during my shower or as I'm getting ready in the morning. But, with all the other things going on at the same time, it's difficult to truly concentrate on my conversation with God.

God wants our undivided attention. Even when Daniel was threatened with death, he still "got down on his knees and prayed, giving thanks to his God, just as he had done before." There was nothing that could separate Daniel from his time with God. Our desire should be to have a prayer life so dedicated that not even death could tear us away from that special time.

Praying Together

Our small group recently had a conversation about praying together as couples. In that discussion, it was revealed that praying couples have a divorce rate of less than one percent! Less than ONE percent! [6] The nationwide divorce rate is estimated to be around 50 percent,[7] even among Christian couples. What is also shocking is that only eight percent of couples pray together on a regular basis.[8]

So why don't we pray together? And I'm just as guilty as the other 92 percent. Is it a fear of opening up? Are we not comfortable praying out loud? I think it's a combination of several things. What I have discovered is that there is a bit of an overall awkwardness involved in praying with your spouse. It's a little uncomfortable, so we just avoid it. But, Jesus said, "...I tell you that if two of you on earth agree about anything you ask for, it will be done for you by my Father in heaven. For where two or three come together in my name, there am I with them."[9]

Stephen Wiskstrom writes:

> *How much do you think you and your spouse could accomplish if you prayed together daily? What would happen to the amount of problems you face as a married couple if you prayed together about them daily? What kind of adults will your children grow into if the two of you prayed together for them daily? Can you see why it is so important for a couple to pray together?*
>
> *When you and your spouse hold hands and pray together, you are coming before God as a couple. It's not just you praying, it's not just your spouse praying, but the two of you praying together. You're united spiritually before God as a team. You are now operating on the level that God intended for couples to operate on. You are unified, joined together as one, partners together before God. Your prayer as a couple is sweet perfume to God.*[10]

Our prayer time together should be in a quiet, undisrupted area as well, where we can be free to speak about anything and be focused on God, our spouse and the prayers on our mind. When we pray together, we open our hearts to each other and to God. Hearing your spouse pray for you will encourage you, and they will be encouraged by hearing your prayers for them. And God is pleased to hear our prayers any time.

Start with something simple. Before bedtime has worked for us, even if we're both not going to sleep at the same time. I may be staying up later to work, or Anne may have had a rough day and headed to bed a little early. Just find a time that works for both of you, and do it. You can start with just three things: pray for your spouse (issues they may be dealing with, situations at work or church, physical pain or suffering); pray for wisdom in your decisions (marriage related decisions, occupational decisions, decisions in raising your children); and pray that your spouse will see Jesus in you.

The Results of United Prayer

Not only will there be positive eternal consequences when we pray together – our children becoming like Christ, our friends finding a relationship with Christ, our own lives growing closer to God – but there will also be earthly consequences as a result of praying together as a couple.

While it may be uncomfortable at times, praying together will open up lines of communication that may not normally be opened. As we pray honestly together, we will be humbled in whatever situation may have caused an argument; we can pray about the issue, instead of dwelling on it as we lay in silence at the end of a tough day.

"Lord, help John to see how wrong he was," is not a good example of praying together honestly. Each of us must be honest with ourselves and our spouse in prayer. Pray for humility. Pray for an attitude of Christ. Pray that your spouse will experience the love of Christ through your actions, thoughts and words. Pray for unity as a husband and wife, as a mother and father. Your daily lives will produce positive results because of it.

Following the lead of Christ in prayer is essential for maintaining a relationship with your spouse that is growing closer and closer to God in every way. If you truly want to secure your marriage and protect it from the nasty grip of divorce, become a praying couple. Allow God into your marriage on a deeper level and see what happens!

From the Chapter

"While it may be uncomfortable at times, praying together will open up lines of communication that may not normally be opened."

Bible Verse Reference

Matthew 18:20 – "For where two or three come together in my name, there am I with them."

Question:

Will you be so bold as to pray this prayer with your husband or wife tonight before you go to bed: "Father, thank you for giving us the perfect example to follow in your son, Jesus Christ. Please guide us in our marriage, that we will strive to become more like you every day. Make us stronger together. Thank you. Amen."

Chapter 10

Do It Joyfully

"I will be satisfied with seeing your likeness." (Psalm 17:15)

I was watching my son the other day as he was driving around in his battery operated Hummer® in front of our house. It was a special day because the Hummer had been in "the shop" (a.k.a. my office) getting fixed for most of the summer, so this was the first time that Isaac was able to ride it in quite some time. I brought it home from the office and was unloading it from the van as Isaac stood excitedly just outside of the garage. Finally, he had his toy back and was ready to conquer the sidewalks once again!

He probably drove that thing for five hours throughout that day. Taking friends for rides. Driving his sister around the block. If I had asked him to run to the grocery store, I'm sure he would have not hesitated. He was having so much fun, it didn't matter what he was doing as long as it involved riding in the Hummer. And, even as he was "helping" his sister by driving her over to the neighbor's house on an errand, there was pure joy in his eyes.

That's when it hit me. We need to approach this goal of being like Jesus in our marriage like Isaac did everything in his little truck...with great joy. We have this wonderful opportunity to show love to our spouse, to show others how Jesus would treat his spouse, and we should take advantage of this opportunity with a gracious attitude. God has given us the example in his son, Jesus Christ. We can grudge along with an attitude of pain and suffering or we can be joyful and thankful that we have the blueprint right in front of us.

From the Inside, Out

Once we look at it this way, we should be excited to get up in the morning to make our spouse coffee. We should jump at the chance to give a back rub, do the dishes, watch the kids, mow the grass, wash the car, speak words of encouragement, say, "I love you."

The excitement has to be genuine, too. God knows your heart. He knows when you're doing or saying something because you feel like it's required. Often times, your spouse can recognize this, too. This joy must come from the inside, out; it must be done out of love and not for show.

I'm not saying it will be easy. In fact, I can assure you it will be difficult. There will be times when this will be the most difficult thing to do – when you're in a bad mood for whatever reason; when your spouse does or says something to set you off; when things just aren't going your way. But, remember the life of Jesus and our ultimate goal of being "like Christ." He didn't allow anything to affect his commitment to serving or his love for others. Even as they hung him on a cross and spit on him and auctioned off his clothes, he said, "Father, forgive them."[1]

As I mentioned in the second chapter, our desire to be like Christ should be a natural reaction to the love and grace God has shown us. This is not a burden, but an opportunity.

Four "Rights"

Having the right attitude is essential to truly become like Jesus in your marriage. We need to do the right thing at the right time in the right way with the right attitude. It's not just about doing the right thing at the right time. It's not just doing the right thing in the right way. It's applying all four "rights" together in every situation. In his book, *The Life You've Always*

Wanted, John Ortberg uses this same description when he talks about being disciplined.

He goes on to say this:

> *A disciplined follower of Jesus is someone who discerns when laughter, gentleness, silence, healing words, or prophetic indignation is called for, and offers it promptly, effectively, and lovingly.[2]*

Several things will happen if we do not have this spirit of joy. We will begin to resent our spouse because we feel like we do so much more than they do. We will start to feel proud about all that we do. We will expect a certain level of reciprocation from our spouse. Our marriage will become a contest around who can collect the most service "points" and then hold them over the other as bargaining chips to get what we want.

On the other hand, if we approach this life of servanthood and Christ-likeness as an opportunity to take our spouse for a ride in the Hummer, the exact opposite is true. We will want to serve because it makes us feel good, and our spouse feels good, too. We will be constantly humbled as we compare ourselves to

Christ and not our spouse or anyone else. The contest will be focused on, "What can I do for you today?" and not, "What can you do for me?"

Pure Joy

C. S. Lewis said, "Joy is the serious business of heaven."[3] And we are to share in this joy as we become Jesus to our spouse. Even when it gets tough, we are to "consider it pure joy."[4]

Ortberg said:

> *Joy is God's basic character. Joy is his eternal destiny.*
> *God is the happiest being in the universe. And God's*
> *intent was that his creation would mirror his joy...As*
> *products of God's creation, creatures made in his*
> *image, we are to reflect God's fierce joy in life.[5]*

Look at each day as an opportunity to reflect God's joy in your marriage. How can you make the goal of becoming more like Jesus into to a fun, life-changing game? See who can be the first to serve the other each day. Who can be most like Jesus throughout the day or week? Find things that can be done anonymously for your spouse – send an anonymous card in the mail with a gift card to a local bookstore or coffee house; hire someone to clean the house at an unexpected time; set up a surprise night out with a friend.

Psalm 17:15 says, "I will be satisfied with your likeness."[6] Let's not wait until we wake up in God's presence in heaven to see his likeness. Let's reflect his likeness to one another in our marriage today. I think Jesus would take his wife for a ride in the Hummer.

From the Chapter

"We have this wonderful opportunity to show love to our spouse, to show others how Jesus would treat his spouse, and we should take advantage of this opportunity with a gracious attitude."

Bible Verse Reference

Psalm 17:15 – "I will be satisfied with seeing your likeness."

Question:

When was the last time you thanked God for sending you the love of your life? Do it now! And, then go take your spouse for a ride in the Hummer – whatever that may mean in your marriage!

Chapter 11

In All Areas

"And whatever you do, whether in word or deed, do it all in the name of the Lord Jesus, giving thanks to God the Father through him." (Col. 3:17)

I never understood the rationale behind a pinch hitter or the justification for having a spot on a team for this position. Granted, I'm not a huge baseball fan, nor do I claim to know too much about the sport. But, here is a guy who has to focus on just one thing in the game of baseball – hitting. Although he must be in good shape in order to run from home plate to first base (or maybe further), he pretty much practices hitting the ball as hard and as far as he possibly can, every day, every day, every day.

At the same time, he's playing along side someone – a short stop, for instance – who not only has to practice hitting, but he also has to practice catching the ball, throwing the ball, responding to different situations on the field, coordinating plays with his teammates, and many other skills associated with being a short stop. If he only focused on one area of his game, say throwing, the other parts of his game would suffer, and he'd be out of a job in a short time. The pinch hitter, on the other hand, just has one thing to do. If he does it well and stays in shape, then he's in a good situation to say the least.

We can't be pinch hitters in our marriage. Doing well in the area of praying with your spouse doesn't make up for a lack of love or a discomfort with servanthood. Jesus didn't focus on just one thing and neither should we as we strive to become more like him.

The characteristics of Jesus should be displayed in every possible area of our marriage. It's not just true for the times when we're trying to be "spiritual." In fact, our lives should not be separated into different categories at all – work, church, home, sports or school. These characteristics should penetrate all of our actions, relationships and words. We must make a valiant effort in all areas of our lives to achieve this goal. Paul says, "And whatever you do, whether in word or deed, do it *all* in the name of the Lord Jesus."

Application for Wives

Wives, displaying the characteristics of Jesus to your husband will look differently for you than it will for him. I

115

don't have to go into all the truths that tell us women and men are different – in the way we think, act, talk, feel. Living in such a way that exemplifies Christ to your husband involves a renewed focus every day to say, "What can I do today to act as Jesus would act toward my husband?"

Show Respect

One of the key phrases for wives from the passage we've read in Ephesians 5 is "the wife must respect her husband." Wives, it is critical that you respect your husband – at home, at work, at church – in everything he does. Disagreeing is one thing, but disrespecting your husband will deteriorate your relationship and his trust and respect for you faster than you could ever imagine.

Paul does not say to wives, "Respect your husband when you agree with what he does." Nor does he say, "Respect your husband in public, but it's okay to put respect aside once you're in your own home." He says wives should respect their husbands, period. One definition of respect is "willingness to show consideration or appreciation."[1] In your quest to be Jesus to your husband, you must show appreciation for your husband and be considerate of his role in the relationship. It is difficult for a husband to love sacrificially if there is not 100% confidence in the respect of his wife.

Submit

Paul says, "Wives, submit to your husbands as to the Lord." There is no negative connotation with the word "submit" as it's used in this context. In fact, it is mentioned in relation to how we are to submit to the Lord. As we discussed in chapter seven, by submitting to your husband as you would submit to God, you are showing your willingness to trust his judgment and your confidence in him as a man, husband and father.

Talk to Him

Communication is integral to a strong marriage, and men are generally not great communicators. So, what does that mean? Wives, you need to help us in this area. Share your thoughts, your hopes and your dreams. Be honest with your husband and open up with regard to your fears and apprehensions. He may not always ask, but tell him anyway. (We'll work on him in the next section!)

Become His Biggest Ally

Study and learn about your husband to understand his goals and desires; then support him in those areas. Become his

117

biggest ally when it comes to his work or school or any other area of his life that he enjoys or spends a great deal of time. Your husband needs to know that, no matter what, you are there for him, supporting him in the daily grind, as well as in his big picture dreams.

Release It to God

It will not be easy to respect, submit, communicate and support your husband every day with a positive attitude. The only thing you can do is release every situation to God and trust that his will be done. God is in control, not you. No matter how talented you are or how hard you try, this cannot be done alone. Allow yourself to let go and let God help you to become more like Christ in every way.

Application for Husbands

Men, at this time I must reveal a profound truth: our wives are different creatures than we are. They think differently. They communicate at different levels than we do. Their emotions are driven by different triggers than ours are. For our wives to see Jesus in us, we have to know them and know what they need. There is not a list of "things to do" to become Jesus to our wives. It will be unique to each marriage, to each couple. But, there are a few areas that will definitely need attention.

Give Her Time

You cannot love your wife sacrificially without spending time with her. If you are to understand your wife and love her in the same way Christ loves the church, you must take the time to be with her. Date nights are a great way to create moments of focused time just for you and your wife. Whether it's a night out or just a quiet night at the house, cherish those times when you can just be with your wife, one on one, and make the most of it by addressing the next couple of areas I'll discuss.

Talk to Her

Christ communicates with the church through his word. It might seem silly to say, but we must also communicate with our wives by using words. This part has never been a real problem for me. I tend to talk too much and have to be told when to shut up. But, for many, talking to your wife is a struggle. You have to make it a priority. Do your best to answer questions with more than just a "yes" or "no." Begin with everyday conversation, and you'll find it easier to share your hopes and dreams.

Listen to Her

As I just mentioned, the talking part is not a problem for me. It's in the listening area that I struggle. When your wife talks, truly listen. To offer a servant's heart, we must know the victories and the pains. We must listen to the details and the dreams. Listening will help you gain a real understanding of her goals and dreams. While opening up and talking is an important step, learning to listen could be the most important of all.

Build Her Up

Our wives need to know that we love them unconditionally, and that we are not here to criticize and condemn them. They need to know that we are here to help them to become what God intends them to be. We are to build up, not tear down. We are to encourage, not discourage.

> *Do not let any unwholesome talk come out of your mouths, but only what is helpful for building others up according to their needs...*[2]

With a Little Help

We cannot do this on our own. Although I mentioned only four areas to focus on for both husbands and wives, taking the steps to actually put these things into practice on a daily basis will be difficult. We must rely on God's strength and the Holy Spirit he has given us as a helper. It's the only way you will make it through the day when your husband comes home forty-five minutes late from work without calling to let you know or when your wife decides the kitchen needs painting on the day of the big game.

We must work together to improve in these areas. Tell your husband or wife that you're going to work on better communication this week, and ask them to help by offering feedback on how you're doing. Ask for suggestions on how to improve in one of these areas. Just knowing that you're trying will be a great step in the right direction.

Don't be just a pinch hitter. Become an all-around athlete when it comes to becoming like Jesus in your marriage. Jesus loved, forgave, served, trusted, encouraged, saved – all at once, all the time. This consistency across all areas of our marriage, this is our goal.

From the Chapter

"We can't be pinch hitters in our marriage. Doing well in the area of praying with your spouse doesn't make up for a lack of love or a discomfort with servanthood. Jesus didn't focus on just one thing and neither should we as we strive to become more like him."

Bible Verse Reference

Colossians 3:17 – "And whatever you do, whether in word or deed, do it all in the name of the Lord Jesus, giving thanks to God the Father through him."

Question:

Which of the four areas discussed in this chapter needs the most attention? Make an effort to work on that this week.

Chapter 12

See the Results

"Thus, by their fruit you will recognize them." (Matthew 7:20)

The big thing these days is reality TV. Every station has one. It has gone beyond just *Survivor* and *American Idol*, although those two still remain very popular. Now, it is *Dancing with the Stars* and *Skating with Celebrities* and many other shows like them. And with these shows comes a new twist – "the results show." This is often on a separate night from the main competition night, where the contestants come back to see who gets sent home based on their performances from the night before.

The results show is always fun because they usually combine the judges' scores with those of the viewing audience, so the actual results often vary from what you might expect. The results show accounts for the judges' evaluation of a performance as well as the votes of the viewing audience.

As with reality TV results shows, people are watching you, making their judgments about you and your marriage. However flawed their perspective may be, they see and hear what they see and hear. They make up their opinions based on their outside view of your performance. The old cliché "perception is reality" certainly applies. However, unlike the results show, there really isn't a joint effort in the judgment of your true character. Only God has the final say.

But, in order to show ourselves as examples of Christ to others, we do need to walk lives worthy of being examined by others. And, when we exemplify Christ in our marriage, the positive results will go far beyond what goes on just between you and your spouse. Your children will witness your love for your spouse. Your friends and neighbors will recognize something different about your relationship. Your relationship with God will improve. And, your outlook on life will be changed.

Your Relationship with God

God desires a relationship with us. As we strive to become more like Jesus, he is thrilled. Spending time in prayer with our spouse is also spending time in communication with God. Humbling ourselves and putting others first makes God happy. Forgiving, loving and uniting with our spouse brings joy to his face.

When I first met Anne, I wanted to get to know her. I wanted to know everything I could about her. Over time, I discovered what she liked or didn't like. I met her friends and got to know her family. As she and I grew closer and closer in our relationship, I also became more connected with her family. As her father saw my enthusiasm and love for his daughter, he also reached out to me and welcomed me into the family.

God works in the same way. As we get to know his son and as we try to become more like him, he reaches out to us even more with his arms open wide.

Your Relationship with Your Spouse

As we've seen throughout this book, the goal of becoming more like Jesus in our marriage is to improve our relationship with our spouse. The goal is not necessarily to make you or your spouse happy, although joy is a likely side affect. The goal is to become stronger together, to grow old together, to be examples to each other and to your children. The goal is to love more, serve more, humble yourself more, pray more, forgive more and be more honest in your marriage.

When we truly put our spouse before ourselves, as Christ did for us on the cross, we will experience the love that God intended for us to experience in our marriage.

Your Relationship with Yourself

When you begin to implement the characteristics of Jesus Christ in your marriage, you will begin to look at things differently. Instead of making decisions based on what is best for you, your thoughts will be driven more by how a decision will affect your spouse. Selfishness, although always present, will be diminished as you open yourself up to the question, "What would Jesus do?" Just like the bracelets from several years ago helped to remind us to think of that question in our everyday lives, this new Christ-like perspective will penetrate our actions and words.

Not only will you treat your spouse with the love, respect and servitude that Jesus would, but you will also notice a change in the way you respond to your children, your coworkers and your friends. Your overall perspective will change as you look at your situations and decisions through God's eyes instead of your own.

Your Relationship with Your Children

What better way to show love to your children than to show love to your spouse in their presence? My eight-year-old is a little less tuned in to all of the little details going on around the house anymore, but Isaac, who is four, continues to amaze me with the things he soaks up when we have no idea he is even in the room. And, I mean "soak up" literally; he is like a little sponge.

Sometimes this can mean we have to be careful what we say when he's around, but on the positive side, we know that he is watching us and soaking in all the good things we are doing to be Jesus to each other in our marriage. Helping me make coffee for Anne in the mornings. Seeing the gentle touches of love in the kitchen at dinner time. Listening to respectful conversation. Our children take in all these things. If we exemplify Christ in these areas, what a great lesson for our children to learn! If our behavior is not worthy of examination, what kind of confusing message are we sending to our kids?

Your Relationship with Others

If we truly display Christ's characteristics in all areas of our marriage, inevitably our friends and neighbors will be

127

exposed to the wonderful relationship that is created as a result. Jesus said:

> *A new command I give you: Love one another. As I have loved you, so you must love one another. By this all men will know that you are my disciples, if you love one another.*[1]

People will see the tenderness and love a husband and wife have for each other after decades of marriage. They will see the relationship of godly headship, submission and respect. They will wonder what's different about you.

There are so many negative things going on in our society today. Marriages are falling apart all around us, both on television and in the real world. We have an opportunity to shine a light into our world. We have an opportunity to show others how a marriage built on the life of Jesus and his relationship with his bride, the church, will not only survive but thrive.

Make It Happen

We are called to be imitators of Christ in our marriage. Jesus has laid out a blueprint for us to follow in Ephesians 5, and throughout the Bible. The instructions are there. All we have to do is make it happen.

It won't be easy. You will feel like it's not possible to live up to the perfect example of Christ. Remember, we just have to commit to doing the best we can to live out our role as a Christian husband or Christian wife, one day at a time. We will fail sometimes, but that's expected. The only true and perfect one is Christ himself. But, if we strive to become more and more like him, with the help of the Holy Spirit in our lives, we will see the difference.

Becoming like Christ in your marriage will not happen over night. It will take persistence. It will take perseverance. It will take flexibility. And, most of all, it will take love...a love that shows your spouse that you are more concerned with his or her needs and desires than your own, a love that forgives, a love full of joy, a love that's truly honest and humble.

And, in the end, that kind of love will make your spouse feel like he or she is *married to Jesus*.

From the Chapter

"The goal is to become stronger together, to grow old together, to be examples to each other and to your children. The goal is to love more, serve more, humble yourself more, pray more, forgive more and be more honest in your marriage."

Bible Verse Reference

John 13:34-35 – "A new command I give you: Love one another. As I have loved you, so you must love one another. By this all men will know that you are my disciples, if you love one another."

Question:

Are you ready to become more like Jesus in your marriage? Start today!

If you haven't been reading this book with your spouse, ask them to read it. If you have, pass it on to someone who would benefit from it.

Know Jesus

Maybe you picked up this book because the title caught your eye, or because someone gave it to you, or maybe it's because you're searching for something to improve or fix your marriage. But, if you've never made a decision to accept Jesus into your life, you may be struggling with some of the concepts in this book. If that is the case, please read through the following and open your heart and mind to what you read. A relationship with God begins this way:

First – Know and believe that God loves you and created you to know him personally. Thank God for his love and plan for your life. John 17:3 says, *"Now this is eternal life: that they may know you, the only true God, and Jesus Christ, whom you have sent."* Jesus said, *"...I came that they may have life, and might have it abundantly."* (John 10:10) The abundant life consists of peace, purpose and fulfillment based on a reconciled relationship with God.

Second – Understand that we are separated from God and cannot know him or experience his plan for our lives because of our sin. The Bible tells us, *"All have sinned and fall short of the glory of God"* (Romans 3:23) and if we die apart from him we will be separated from him for eternity. *"For the wages of sin is death..."* (Romans 6:23)

Third – Rely on Jesus Christ, who died in our place, paying the penalty for our sin and providing the only way to enter into a personal relationship with God and have eternal life in heaven. *"God demonstrates his own love toward us, in that while we were yet sinners, Christ died for us."* (Romans 5:8) Christ speaking: *"I am the way, and the truth, and the life; no one comes to the Father, but through me."* (John 14:6)

Fourth – Receive Jesus Christ as your Savior and Lord by inviting him in and accepting, as a free gift, his death on the cross as payment for your sins. *"But as many as received him, to them he gave the right to become children of God, even to those who believe in his name."* (John 1:12) Ephesians 2:8-9 reads, *"For by grace you have been saved through faith; and that not of yourselves, it is the gift of God; not as a result of works, that no one should boast."*

If you'd like to begin a journey with a loving God who wants to be with you forever, I invite you to pray the following prayer in the sincerity of your heart.

Dear God, I need you. I acknowledge that I have been living my life apart from your perfect plan and purpose for me. Thank you for sending your son, Jesus Christ, to die on the cross for man's sin. I now want to enter into a personal relationship with you by accepting Christ's death on the cross as payment for my own sins. I open the door of my life and receive you as my Savior and Lord. Thank you for forgiving me of all my sins. Take control of my life. Make me the kind of person you want me to be. It's in the name of Jesus that I pray this prayer. Amen.

Here are some of the results of placing your faith in Jesus Christ:

1. Christ comes into your life. (Colossians 1:27)
2. Your sins are forgiven. (Colossians 1:14)
3. You become a child of God. (John 1:12)
4. You receive eternal life. (John 5:24)
5. You have the power to pursue intimacy with God. (Romans 5:5)
6. You begin the great adventure for which God created you. (John 10:10 and 2 Corinthians 5:17)

If you have prayed to receive Christ, you have made the best decision of your life! I encourage you to find a church that teaches the Bible and centers on Christ so that you can learn more about what it means to walk in harmony with God.

Once you have made this decision and begun the journey, your goal to become more like Jesus in your marriage will take on much greater importance. Your recognition of Christ's ultimate sacrifice for you will encourage, not discourage, your love and sacrifice for your spouse.

Congratulations! Welcome to the journey.

(This section used with permission by Athletes in Action, *"Real People, Real Faith."* Athletes in Action. Xenia, Ohio. 2003)

Sources

Preface
1. Pinckney, Coty. *What is Christian Marriage?* (sermon) Community Bible Church: Williamstown, MA, 1997
2. the Lord your God: Joshua 1:9

Chapter 1
1. Whatever you do: Colossians 3:17
2. example that you should do: John 13:15
3. For what I do: Romans 7:19
4. Anyone who loves: Matthew 10:37
5. Submit to one another: Ephesians 5:21-33
6. the Holy Spirit: John 14:26-27
7. Pinckney, Coty. *What is Christian Marriage?* (sermon) Community Bible Church: Williamstown, MA, 1997
8. the fruit of the Spirit: Galatians 5:22-23
9. Therefore, as God's chosen people: Colossians 3:12-14
10. A new command: John 13:34-35
11. Description of Jesus' death: Warren, Rick. The Purpose Driven Life. Grand Rapids: Zondervan, 2002
12. My command is this: John 15:12-13

Chapter 2
1. Definition of Grace: *The American Heritage® Dictionary of the English Language, Fourth Edition, Copyright © 2000 by Houghton Mifflin Company. Published by Houghton Mifflin Company. All rights reserved.*
2. For it is by grace: Ephesians 2:8-10
3. What good is it: James 2:14-17
4. As the body without the Spirit is dead: James 2:26

135

5. Rich Mullins. "Screen Door." *Songs*. BMG Songs, Inc., 1986.

6. every good tree: Matthew 7:17-20

7. Michael W. Smith. Give It Away." *Change Your World*. Reunion Records, 1992.

8. by their fruit: Matthew 7:20

Chapter 3

1. Pinckney, Coty. *What is Christian Marriage*? (sermon) Community Bible Church: Williamstown, MA, 1997

2. The wife's body: 1 Corinthians 7:4

3. Pinckney, Coty. *What is Christian Marriage*? (sermon) Community Bible Church: Williamstown, MA, 1997

4. But, God demonstrates: Romans 5:8

5. Pinckney, Coty. *What is Christian Marriage*? (sermon) Community Bible Church: Williamstown, MA, 1997

6. Pinckney, Coty. *What is Christian Marriage*? (sermon) Community Bible Church: Williamstown, MA, 1997

7. My command is this: John 15:12-13

Chapter 4

1. For even the Son of Man: Mark 10:45

2. Ortberg, John. *The Life You've Always Wanted*. Grand Rapids: Zondervan, 1997, 2002

3. so he got up from the meal: John 13:4-5

4. Each one should use whatever gift: 1 Peter 4:10

5. Ortberg, John. *The Life You've Always Wanted*. Grand Rapids: Zondervan, 1997, 2002

6. Do you understand: John 13:12-17

Chapter 5

1. *Liar, Liar*. dir. Tom Shadyac. Universal Studios, 1997.

2. Do not let any unwholesome talk: Ephesians 4:29

3. Bonhoffer, Deitrich. *Life Together*, New York: Harper & Row, 1956

4. How good is a timely word: Proverbs 15:23

5. If we confess: 1 John 1:9

6. Ortberg, John. *The Life You've Always Wanted.* Grand Rapids: Zondervan, 1997, 2002

7. Ortberg, John. *The Life You've Always Wanted.* Grand Rapids: Zondervan, 1997, 2002

8. Ortberg, John. *The Life You've Always Wanted.* Grand Rapids: Zondervan, 1997, 2002

Chapter 6

1. seventy times seven: Matthew 18:22

2. At that point Peter got up: Matthew 18:21-35. Scripture taken from *The Message*. Copyright © 1993, 1994, 1995, 1996, 2000, 2001, 2002. Used by permission of NavPress Publishing Group.

3. For if you forgive men: Matthew 6:14-15

4. And when you stand praying: Mark 11:25

5. Father, forgive them: Luke 23:34

6. Warren, Rick. The Purpose Driven Life. Grand Rapids: Zondervan, 2002

Chapter 7

1. Your attitude should be: Philippians 2:5-8

2. Ortberg, John. *The Life You've Always Wanted.* Grand Rapids: Zondervan, 1997, 2002

3. Ortberg, John. *The Life You've Always Wanted.* Grand Rapids: Zondervan, 1997, 2002

4. Submit to one another: Ephesians 5:21-33

5. Pinckney, Coty. *What is Christian Marriage*? (sermon) Community Bible Church: Williamstown, MA, 1997

6. Do not think of yourself: Romans 12:3-5

7. If one part: 1 Corinthians 12:26

8. Pinckney, Coty. *What is Christian Marriage?* (sermon) Community Bible Church: Williamstown, MA, 1997

Chapter 8
1. For this reason: Genesis 2:24
2. Pinckney, Coty. *What is Christian Marriage?* (sermon) Community Bible Church: Williamstown, MA, 1997
3. husbands ought to love: Ephesians 5:28-29, 33
4. Let us make man in our image: Genesis 1:26-27
5. I appeal to you: 1 Corinthians 1:10
6. How good and pleasant: Psalm 133:1

Chapter 9
1. This then is how you should pray: Matthew 6:9-13
2. And when you pray: Matthew 6:5-8
3. Very early in the morning: Mark 1:35
4. Going a little further: Matthew 26:39
5. Warren, Rick. *The Purpose Driven Life.* Grand Rapids: Zondervan, 2002
6. Praying couples divorce rate: Ruhnke, Robert A. *For Better and For Ever.* San Antonio: 2000.
7. Nationwide divorce rate: Ruhnke, Robert A. *For Better and For Ever.* San Antonio: 2000.
8. Praying couples: Rainey, Dennis. *Prayer: The Secret to a Lasting Marriage.* Little Rock. FamilyLife.com.
9. I tell you that if two of you: Matthew 18:19-20
10. Wiskstrom, Stephen. *Praying Together as a Couple.* CrossMap.com, 2004.

Chapter 10
1. Father, forgive them: Luke 23:34
2. Ortberg, John. *The Life You've Always Wanted.* Grand Rapids: Zondervan, 1997, 2002

3. Lewis, C.S. *Letters to Malcolm, Chiefly on Prayer*. New York: Harcourt, Brace & World, 1964
4. Consider it pure joy: James 1:2
5. Ortberg, John. *The Life You've Always Wanted*. Grand Rapids: Zondervan, 1997, 2002
6. I will be satisfied: Psalm 17:15

Chapter 11
1. Respect. (n.d.). *The American Heritage® Dictionary of the English Language, Fourth Edition*. Retrieved September 20, 2006, from Dictionary.com website:
http://dictionary.reference.com/search?q=respect&x=53&y=14
2. Do not let any unwholesome talk: Ephesians 4:29

Chapter 12
1. A new command: John 13:34-35